NIGHT INTRUDER

NIGHT INTRUDER

A personal account of the radar war between
the RAF and Luftwaffe nightfighter forces

JEREMY HOWARD-WILLIAMS

DAVID & CHARLES

NEWTON ABBOT   LONDON

NORTH POMFRET (VT)   VANCOUVER

To
ROSEMARY and VIOLETTE
each of whom bravely lent me her husband
for nearly two years

ISBN 0 7153 7054 5
Library of Congress Catalog Card Number 75–31314

Set in 11 on 13pt Baskerville
and printed in Great Britain
by Latimer Trend & Company Ltd Plymouth
for David & Charles (Publishers) Limited
Brunel House Newton Abbot Devon

Published in the United States of America
by David & Charles Inc
North Pomfret Vermont 05053 USA

Published in Canada
by Douglas David & Charles Limited
1875 Welch Street North Vancouver BC

CONTENTS

LIST OF ILLUSTRATIONS

7

FOREWORD

As a former Luftwaffe nightfighter pilot, I have read this book with much interest and pleasure. It is a fine document of the great and thrilling experience of flying, and of the exciting challenge of night flying in particular. As a gifted pilot, Jeremy Howard-Williams has been able to record the interesting development and the practical use of electronic devices designed to search and find aircraft in pitch-dark night, in thick clouds, and in fog. But he has not drawn a one-sided picture from the RAF angle only, as he writes also of German radar and related electronic techniques.

I have found much in this book to show that the problems and experiences were very much the same on either side of the fence. The human side of the story holds many similarities as well. We were so wonderfully young—and sometimes foolish— in those days. But, despite the stupidity of war, we at least can say that we did pioneering work for all of aviation, pushing ahead instrument and bad-weather flying, and promoting the electronic development that has resulted in the devices now in use for peaceful air-traffic control for airliners.

May this fine book help to further reconciliation between our nations and bring about understanding, and friendship, in a United Europe to come.

RUDOLF ALEXANDER SCHOENERT

Rudolf Schoenert was Commanding Officer of the Luftwaffe's nightfighter experimental unit Nachtjagd Gruppe 10 at Werneuchen, which was the exact equivalent of the Fighter

9

Interception Development Squadron of which Jeremy Howard-Williams was Flight Commander. He was there from 1 January 1944 until 28 February 1945 and was then promoted to major and made group commander of Nachtjagd Gruppe 5, where he finished the war; he was credited with the destruction of sixty-four aircraft. The author was at FIDS from 31 August 1943 until 12 April 1945 and therefore he and Rudolf Schoenert were exact opposite numbers.

INTRODUCTION

This is two stories in one. It is a personal account of night fighting between the RAF and the Luftwaffe in World War II. Being personal, it also portrays the kind of daily life we led and it tries to show some of the human factors which entered into the game. I have used this as an excuse to include a couple of family adventures (on the BE 2e and Spitfire), neither of which has anything to do with night fighting; with one son on day fighters and the other taking over at night, my mother probably had a rougher war than either of us realised at the time . . .

I am aware that the style is somewhat dated, but it is a document of the period and I felt that it would be wrong to write it out of character. If we sound like overgrown schoolboys, this is because that is precisely what we were. We cost a lot of time, effort and money to train, so we were somewhat pampered at squadron level; this inevitably went to our heads a bit. We were living an artificial existence in which we could expect death at any moment, so we played a game of make-believe. We drank a lot of beer and talked about Huns, popsies, wizard prangs, stooging about and the chop rate; we also worked for more than half of every day (and sometimes much longer), seven days a week.

This book would have been the poorer without the help of many people. Don Spurgeon was a mine of information on various forms of airborne radar. Mr Hine of the Imperial War Museum was most helpful over photographs, as were Fokkers and Messerschmitt-Bölkow-Blohm. Horst Diener, the Luftwaffe's Referent für Nachtjagd, also helped with some of the photographs and put me in touch with my opposite number in the wartime German Air Force. In 1944 Rudolph Schoenert commanded NJG 10 at Werneuchen, the Luftwaffe's night-fighter trials unit, which was so similar to the Fighter Interception Unit; I am indebted to him for his kind Foreword and can but echo the words of his last paragraph.

Finally, I must say thank you to Tony and Mac, both of whom kindly read the typescript and prodded my memory here and there. I suppose one tends to take people for granted, but not any more as far as these two are concerned. At the wedding where the photograph on page 104 was taken, one of the other guests turned to me.

'I knew you and Mac were friends,' she said. 'But I never realised you were so close.'

My Scotsman and I had been through much together, but I never knew it showed.

Warsash 1976   J. N. H-W

1 THE PROBLEM

AI stands for Airborne Interception and was the way in which radar, carried in nightfighters for locating the enemy, was referred to by the RAF during World War II. I made my first acquaintance with AI while undergoing elementary flying training on the Tiger Moth aircraft at Sealand in the spring of 1941. On the far side of the airfield black Beaufighters were being wheeled in and out of a hangar for a most secret modification, about which nobody was allowed to speak. It was, in fact, AI Mk IV and I was to gain a better knowledge of it later in the year.

But first I went from Sealand to Canada where, to my horror, I found that I was to fly the twin-engined Avro Anson. I say 'to my horror' because this was a sign that I was almost certainly destined for Bomber Command, but it was my firm resolve to become a day-fighter pilot on Spitfires like my elder brother, who at that time was serving as a flying officer with 118 Squadron at Ibsley in the south of England. He shot down his first enemy aircraft while I was in Canada and my diary waxed lyrical.

27 August 1941
A letter arrives from Peter telling me that he has shot down his first Hun officially confirmed; apparently it was an ME 109. Good for him. His letter does not give enough details for my liking, but I am able to supply these myself when I proudly tell the others about my big brother. It gives me quite a lift to be able to shoot this particular line, but it seems I overdo it because I start telling the same people twice and they begin to get annoyed.

Before you get the impression that I was a crusading hero with a burning desire to throw myself into the hottest action, let me quickly make it clear that it was with considerable trepidation that, at the age of eighteen in 1940, I joined the services at all.

The combination of a vivid imagination and a certain amount of intelligence is one which can be disquieting to an active mind. It is imagination which conjures up the pain, the fear of wounds, the loneliness of dying. And it is imagination which strips the flesh from the soul as you picture your acquaintances with nothing better to do than put a microscope on your movements and motivations while you hesitate on the brink. Eventually, of course, imagination creates a conflict within you between the fear of fright and the fear of being seen to be afraid. To this conflict there can be but one outcome and, after Dunkirk, it became impossible for me to continue as a civilian in the knowledge that all my friends were serving.

Having screwed up my courage to profess an outward desire to get to grips with my country's enemies, it was somewhat galling to be constantly confronted with barriers to this goal. It was almost as though somebody was saying: 'All right, you've made your point. Now crawl back into your funkhole and be thankful.' I started out as a ground defence airman (a sort of permanent airfield sentry), which caused me after three frustrating months to appeal to my father for the only time in my service career—he was an air commodore at the time—to help me get my foot on to the bottom rung of the ladder which led me eventually to the pilot's cockpit. Next, my flying abilities in Canada appeared to please the authorities, for they offered me the chance of staying on at the school and becoming an instructor. But I had professed such a public desire to get on to operations that it was not possible to back down with any grace, nor with a clear conscience, no matter how great the temptation. So back to England I came, not to the Spitfires I wanted but, because my training had been on twin-engined aircraft and I had expressed such a forceful wish to get on to fighters, to twin-engined fighters—in short, to nightfighters. On the same day came the news that Peter had been awarded the DFC; his score was now three ME 109s destroyed.

In Germany at this time, the star of a certain Luftwaffe general was in the ascendant. Promoted from colonel on return from a prisoner-of-war camp in France in July 1940, General Kammhuber had been given the task of forming the Luftwaffe's first nightfighter division. He started with a Messerschmitt 110 Gruppe (I/ZG.1) and various Junkers 88 fighter and Dornier 17 intruder flights. By 1 August 1941 the force had expanded sufficiently to be redesignated as a corps and Kammhuber was beginning to get the ground radar with the communications and control system he so urgently needed. What is more, nine days later the first British bomber was intercepted and brought to visual range at night using *Lichtenstein* AI airborne radar. Although the Germans had been developing radar since before the war (a fact unknown to us and not, for a long time, accepted by many of our scientists), they were behind us—and were to remain so throughout the war—in its airborne application. Luftwaffe reaction to *Lichtenstein* was lukewarm, but Kammhuber knew that it had to come and was delighted with this first success.

My operational training was to be at No 54 OTU (Operational Training Unit) at Church Fenton using the Bristol Blenheim, a twin-engined aircraft then being phased out of operations. It was said that you could always tell a Blenheim pilot by the callouses on his knuckles, caused by barking them continuously on bits of projecting metal as he groped vainly behind him for the various inconveniently positioned knobs, wheels and levers used for altering airscrew pitch, changing fuel tanks, trimming the aircraft, altering the setting of the engine-cooling gills or raising and lowering the undercarriage and flaps—known collectively to aircrew as the 'tits'.

Both on Tiger Moths and Ansons, I had made a nodding acquaintance with the factor which was almost as much a threat to a pilot's life as the Germans: what goes up must come down. Gravity, or rather Sir Isaac Newton, claimed an ever-increasing toll of victims throughout the war, especially those who were called upon to fly regardless of weather—and we shall see later how nightfighters came to be the first of the all-weather fighters. It was, I suppose, a defence mechanism to endow with a personality the threat of crashing as the result either of bad weather or plain finger trouble in failing to fly properly on instruments, so we referred to it as 'Sir Isaac' or, on the occasions when we thought he wasn't listening, as plain 'Isaac'.

Instrument flying is always more difficult when you are cold and tired. The aircraft plunges into an all-pervading impersonal mass of greyness from which all static reference points are removed. The wise pilot lowers his seat and gets his head down to the then relatively primitive instrument panel without further ado, and stays there until he is quite sure that he can see a genuine horizon of some kind (and not a false horizon caused by an oblique line of clouds, which would get him off on the wrong foot).

The aircraft is buffeted by turbulence, which can reach alarming proportions, especially in the upper parts of cumulus cloud. Constant corrections to the controls are necessary and complete faith must be placed in the instruments. This may not sound difficult but, when your every sense is screaming out that you are flying straight and level yet the blind-flying panel says you are in a diving turn, it is not always easy to believe the story it tells. But you *must* believe it and force yourself to take corrective action quickly or you will soon be dead. When the instruments then say that you have regained level flight, you may think that you are skidding or turning. What has happened is that your balance motors, working by means of fluid and sensory hairs in the tubes in the ears, are actuated by gravity and can be fooled by centrifugal force.

While all this is going on, Sir Isaac's faithful henchmen do their best to distract your attention. Rain and hail beat on the windscreen and fuselage, electrical discharge is manifested by ripples of lightning running up and down the windscreen and forming rings of fire round the tips of the propellers; ice builds

up on the leading edge of the wings, engine cowlings, radio
aerials and propeller blades, until it starts to destroy the aero-
foil shape of your aircraft with resulting loss of lift, chokes the
engine air intake thus reducing power, spoils electrical insula-
tion and thus ruins radio reception, or bits fly off and hit the
fuselage with thuds and bangs.

Darkness is complete.

Cold and tiredness strike at your morale, you hope you will
find room beneath cloud to break clear of the opaque dampness
in which visibility is not more than the end of the wing tip,
before you hit the ground, and you continue to fight the controls. Some of us had to work harder at it than others. To many,
instrument flying was fraught with danger and worry, to be
wrestled with and held at bay but never fully understood and
certainly never overcome; to some it was a mechanical exercise
which nevertheless required constant and assiduous application
with an iron self-discipline. The fortunate few were able to
dismiss it as a purely secondary function while the main task of
the particular flight took place; but everybody needed to keep
in practice.

Sir Isaac was a very real threat which gradually receded as a
pilot gained experience and ability, only to recur a good deal
later when the effects of strain began to show. This was because
most pilots suffered one or two near misses during their career,
or saw those suffered by their friends, and got to thinking about
life generally. And when you start to think about life it is a
short step to thinking about death, which was always just round
the corner, particularly when the weather was bad. Known to
the authorities as 'operational fatigue' or, in extreme cases, 'lack
of moral fibre' (LMF for short), aircrew used to refer to this
state of mind as 'the twitch'. Some of us got it early and some
got it late, but it came to most of us sooner or later, depending
on how quickly one's personal batteries became discharged.
Everyone drew from his batteries to keep going and usually
nobody else knew how near to the reserve each man was getting. The system of a rest period between tours of operations

was designed to allow aircrew to recharge their batteries every eighteen months or so. To help stave off a completely flat battery before a tour of operations was complete, aircrew were a pampered lot. We had eggs for night-flying supper, half a pint of milk every day, orange juice when it was available and a special allowance of petrol granted purely for recreational purposes (I had to try and explain this once to an extremely doubting policeman). There were a hundred and one other perks which we took for granted, and I wonder how many times some humble airman waiting to have an aching tooth filled was put back yet another month, so that some pilot or navigator could walk straight in and be attended to right away.

While flying with a squadron we worked seven days a week and quite often eighteen or more hours a day; our leave allowance was liberal, being a week every three months or so with a 48-hour pass between each leave. We spent our leaves in widely differing ways of course, for what was relaxation to one man was anathema to another. I can recall one pilot who used to spend every night of his leaves in night clubs and came back to us pale and worn, yet entirely mentally refreshed. I usually used to go to my home just outside Bath, where my mother was being given a home for the duration by her sister. There I would walk, do a little shooting and sleep (on one 48-hour pass I slept for exactly half the time, while my mother apparently rushed about downstairs saying little more than 'Sssh'). All this was designed to postpone the effects of the twitch. This was a secret struggle which went on in all of us. To some the showdown came sooner, to some later; some won it; some lost it; some gave up the struggle; some had it postponed by a rest from operations. For others Sir Isaac himself solved the problem, others were just plain lucky. But let me make one thing clear, no man who has fought that struggle would ever question the actions of a fellow-struggler who may, perhaps, have suffered greater stress, real or imagined. No man who has not fought it has the right to pass judgement.

There had been fatal accidents on both the flying courses I

had so far attended. It seemed reasonable to suppose that there would be more as the aircraft got more complicated and as the Luftwaffe thought it more worth while to intrude into our night-flying circuits. The Blenheim was not a difficult aeroplane to fly, but it was a good deal heavier and faster than the rather staid Anson, which was of a forgiving nature. You had to control a Blenheim, an Anson would fly itself. An indication of the accident rate was given, had we but known it, by our reception at No 54 OTU. The Sergeants' and Officers' Messes were always full to capacity on the arrival of a course. It was quite usual for aircrew to be billeted out or even put under canvas and, on their protest, to be assured that there would be room in the Mess within a week. What they weren't told was that these vacancies were caused either by Sir Isaac taking personal control of an aircraft in bad weather, or else by the close attentions of the Luftwaffe. I arrived on 21 October 1941, not knowing anything about this and also not knowing that Hitler himself had issued an order the week before, revoking permission for the Luftwaffe to mount intruder operations. British aircraft, he said, must be destroyed over Germany where the public could see them coming down, and not over England—even though the scoring rate of the latter was far better from the German point of view.

12 November 1941
First solo on the Blenheim. I climb into the cockpit, check all round, open the cowling gills, see that the hydraulic lever is switched to work the undercarriage and flaps (and not the gun turret), that the undercarriage lever is down, the fuel selected to tanks with adequate supplies, the propellers in fine pitch, the fuel-mixture control is on rich and the flaps up. I switch on and stick my head out of the port window to call to the groundcrew who are operating the external battery—the trolley acc as it is known.

'Contact port!' The cry is repeated. I press the tit and the engine roars into life. I adjust the throttle and then my thumb goes up and I point to the starboard engine. The mechanic imitates the signal to show that all

is well and the other engine starts. The trolley acc is unplugged and wheeled away and I glance over the various instruments while I am waiting for the engines to warm up.

A second check on the hydraulic selector lever and I then put down my hand to exercise the flaps, taking care not to confuse levers with the under-carriage; the two controls are side by side and, of all stupid arrangements, have almost identical levers. I look down to ensure that I have the correct one and then operate the flaps successfully. I press button A on the R/T (radio telephone) control box to get flying-control frequency. As soon as the set is warmed up I run each engine in turn up to zero boost and check for excessive drop in revs as I switch each magneto off in turn; we are allowed a 50 rpm drop, providing the engine isn't too rough.

Having found the revs OK, with oil pressures and temperatures at correct figures, I stretch over my left shoulder and put each propeller into coarse pitch and watch the drop in revolutions. When I have returned the levers to the fine position I am ready to check the brake pressure and wave away the chocks from the wheels.

'Hello Marker, this is Circus 62 calling. Permission to taxi out please. Over.'

'Hello 62.' Flying control answer my call immediately; they have been warned that this is a first solo. 'Marker here. OK to taxi to east/west runway. Listening out.'

I taxi carefully out and stop on the perimeter track just short of the beginning of the runway.

'PMCRAFTS,' I mutter to myself, quoting the mnemonic for the cockpit check before take-off.

P.   Petrol on and enough. Pitot head heater on.

M.   Mixture rich.

C.   Cylinder-head temperatures OK.

R.   Retractibles: hydraulics off turret and on wheels and flaps.

A.   Airscrew fully fine; throttle nut tight.

F.   Flaps up.

T.   Trim: rudder neutral, elevator slightly nose down.

S.   Sperry gyro set to compass heading.

'Good. Now close the engine gills.' I glance up and see that nothing else is coming in to land.

'Hello Marker, Circus 62 calling. Permission to scramble please, over.'

'Hello 62, Marker here. OK to scramble. Listening out.'

I taxi forward to the runway. For the first hundred yards or so it is grass, as the tarmac strip has not been extended right to the perimeter track.

'I'd better wait until I get properly on the runway before I open up,' I think. Then I change my mind. 'No. I'll start now, I won't be going fast by the time the tarmac starts.'

I open the throttles and the Blenheim immediately leaps forward.

'Too fast for this grass,' I think, and start to throttle back. 'Too late. I'll be going fast anyway, so I'd better rush it.' I push the throttles fully open and hang on for dear life. The Blenheim leaps about over the uneven surface and I am a little scared. The beginning of the tarmac runway soon arrives and the aircraft bounces sharply. It swerves over to the right and then straightens up as I apply left rudder.

My starboard wheel is now off the runway and bouncing along the grass on the right. The rest of the aeroplane is on the tarmac surface, but I decide to press on with my take-off. The Blenheim is bucking about and gathering speed rapidly. I manage to hold it straight and notice with dismay a crowd of workmen looming up in front. Shortly before we reach them at the end of the runway the aeroplane takes the air. This it does with no conscious effort of mine and we swing crazily away, climbing slowly.

My next actions are completely automatic. Wheels up. Throttle back to cruising boost. Propellers into coarse pitch. The aircraft proceeds to fly me round the sky for the next five minutes, during which time I am content just to sit at the controls.

'OK Jesus, I've got her.' I come out of my semi-coma and grin to myself at the old joke about the Good Lord taking control for the first five minutes of a first solo, which I can now better understand having been a perfect illustration of it. I resume control and discover that I am sweating freely. The take-off has frightened me considerably and I am glad to have got safely out of it. The Blenheim gives the impression of having a good deal more metal about it than any aeroplane I have yet flown. It is all sharp corners inside and already my knuckles are cut and bruised from

operating the inconveniently placed tits. It passes through my mind that a crash in one of these could have unpleasant consequences. (I am to try this out at first hand before the end of the course, only to prove that the Blenheim is, fortunately, not a killer every time.)

After an hour, during which time I manage to cool off a little, I wipe myself down thoroughly so as not to reveal my state to the groundcrew (as if they could be fooled), return to the airfield and make an uneventful landing.

After learning to fly the Blenheim by day, we then had to move into D Squadron to fly it by night and to team up with a radio operator before starting to find out all about AI. The electronic equipment, which was later christened radar by the Americans —from the initial letters of RAdio Direction And Range— was at that time known publicly as radiolocation in England, but the fact that we had radar in aircraft had not been released.

The equipment in squadron use was AI Mk IV, which transmitted radio pulses all round the fighter aircraft, thus 'floodlighting' the surrounding airspace. This restricted its maximum

---

Fig 1   *AI Mk IV display*

In AI Mk IV, a dipole aerial fixed in the nose of the aircraft broadcast radio waves on $1\frac{1}{2}$m, in pulses to 'floodlight' the sky all round the fighter aircraft. Receiving dipoles were positioned above and below either wing, so that they could measure the difference in the return time of the radar pulse as it echoed back from any large object which was covered by the radiations. These time differences (only microsec) were suitably displayed on two cathode-ray tubes in the navigator's cockpit, and showed the angle off in both elevation and azimuth.

Because the transmitter floodlighted the sky, it follows that the ground beneath the fighter received as many pulses as did the sky in front. This meant that a massive return echo was received from the ground, at a range equal to the fighter aircraft's height, which effectively drowned out any smaller target such as another aircraft, if it were beyond that range. Thus, a fighter equipped with AI Mk IV which was flying at just over 5,000ft altitude had a maximum radar range of one mile, while at 21,000ft this went up to four miles. Normal minimum range was about 800–1,000ft.

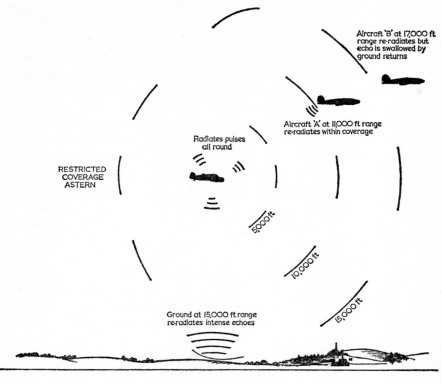

Aircraft 'B' at 17,000 ft range re-radiates but echo is swallowed by ground returns

Aircraft 'A' at 11,000 ft range re-radiates within coverage

Radiates pulses all round

RESTRICTED COVERAGE ASTERN

5,000 ft

10,000 ft

15,000 ft

Ground at 15,000 ft range re-radiates intense echoes

AI Mk IV DISPLAY

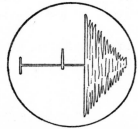

Elevation tube shows range as well. The ground returns are to the right and indicate altitude. The fighter is flying at about 15,000 ft, and the target is 30° up at 11,000 ft range.

Azimuth tube shows range as well. Target is dead ahead at 11,000 ft range. At lower altitude the 'Christmas tree' effect would be nearer the direct pulse at the bottom of the time base.

range to the height of the fighter, because the ground beneath sent back a massive echo which swamped the set from that range outwards. Any aircraft flying closer than the fighter's height, therefore, would send back an echo which could be seen in the clear part of the cathode-ray tubes. It was then the radio operator's job to interpret the signals he saw and to instruct the pilot what to do: turn right or left, climb or dive, speed up or slow down.

Before you get the impression that this is easy, let me remind you that the AI sets of those days were far from perfect and were constantly breaking down or giving false readings. Even if the set were working well and the target nicely within range, the RO saw indications on his CRTs telling him only roughly how many degrees the target was off the centreline of the fighter, both in the azimuth and elevation planes. He had no direct indication of which way the target was heading or whether it was in the act of turning, accelerating or slowing down; all this information he had to infer from change of angle and change of range. Even in those days things happened quickly enough to make it vital to give the order where to go first, followed by how quickly to do the manoeuvre and then information on the target's movements, thus:

'Left, hard left. Tighten the turn, he's crossing starboard to port range about two miles. Ease the turn. Steady. He's 5° port and 5° up. Range still two miles. Port again gently. Steady. Dead ahead now, still slightly up, throttle back a bit, range coming down rather fast.'

So you can see that choice of RO was vital. My diary sums up the problem nicely.

7 December 1941
Moved into D Squadron. Look around the new dispersal hut on arrival and note about twenty sergeants sitting around reading. ROs presumably. I look at them all, wondering whether I shall ever resolve these indistinguishable faces into human beings with different personalities. A lot depends on my choice of RO because for the next two years we shall live,

fly and fight together; we must be a sympathetic team. Possibly we shall die together.

My fellow-officer pupils and I decide that the NCO pilots will have picked all the best ROs already, because they all live in the Sergeants' Mess together and get first choice. We resolve to make a careful inspection of the available talent. But my ego is pricked somewhat by a young sergeant coming up and asking me whether I am yet 'crewed up'. This is so different from what I had expected, where I would be the one to do the choosing, that I am taken aback. I look at him keenly and what I see pleases me. The sergeant is a slight man of about my own height, which is 5ft 9in. Even a large black moustache cannot hide his youth, but he has a nice-looking candour about his features. Blue eyes set wide apart are looking me straight in the face and seem ready to smile easily. His voice is pleasant and educated, and he sounds fluent (an important factor in anyone required to give a running commentary during an interception). We agree to take each other on trial, from which either can opt out at any time.

However, we never refer to this option again and I, for one, never have cause to think about it any more; I certainly never regret our collaboration. I can't say that I liked the thought of having the responsibility of a married man on my hands, but I was to receive much kindness and a touch of home from Rosemary and Tony over the next two years. Their union was the old-fashioned kind which lasts and today they run an inn at St Dogmaels, South Wales, together; I am proud to have been godfather to their daughter.

While we were in D Squadron we had a visit from Lord Trenchard, the Father of the Royal Air Force. He was a sort of unofficial Inspector General and a legendary figure since the days of World War I. He brought some photographs with him of damage caused by one of the recent Bomber Command attacks on Germany. The centre of this particular town had been razed to the ground and he asked us if we noticed anything particular about the damage. I was lucky enough to spot that all the bridges were still intact and mentioned this.

'That's right, my boy.' He looked up from the prints over which we were all leaning. 'What's your name?'

'Howard-Williams, sir,' I replied.

'Relation?' The deep voice barked the one word, as piercing eyes queried me from under his shaggy brows.

'Yes, sir. He's my father.'

Was it imagination or was there a hint of approval in the grunt he gave as he turned to the next photograph? He must have drawn some satisfaction from the knowledge that the next generation were following their fathers' footsteps.

31 December 1941
Pat has joined the WAAF and been posted to York. I hadn't seen her since March 1939, when we were students together in France, until two days ago. We join Tony and Rosemary for a double celebration: New Year's Eve and, more important, Tony's RO wings newly awarded. Pat and I kept putting Yours *on the gramophone until the rest of the diners must have been sick of the sound of Vera Lynn's voice.*

Luck was with us at Church Fenton for, apart from a wheels-up landing Tony and I had one night in a Blenheim, we got through our training well enough for our request to go to 604 Squadron at Middle Wallop to be accepted, much to my astonishment. This was the crack nightfighter unit of the RAF and was commanded by the redoubtable Wing Commander John Cunningham (later Group Capt. Cunningham, CBE, DSO, DFC, DL, Chief Test Pilot to de Havillands). His standards were high and anyone who failed to come up to them was usually posted overseas, where there was a constant demand for crews. In their early days at 604, new pilots felt that there was a troopship permanently alongside the dock labelled 'Reserved for 604 Squadron. Destination: Middle East.'

2   604 SQUADRON

27 January 1942

Tony and I arrive at Middle Wallop to report for duty. The Beau-fighter Mk I is fitted with Hercules XI radial engines and I immediately fall in love with this aeroplane. The cockpit is as well laid out as the Blenheim's was bad, and everything lies under the hand which has to use it.

On take-off, the left hand opens the throttles (right throttle a little in advance of the left, to counteract swing) and merely has to move forward a few inches to raise the undercarriage lever and can then immediately return to the throttles to make sure that they don't creep back at this critical stage of a flight. Switches are thoughtfully arranged so that they are split into small groups; this means that the pilot can identify each switch at night by feel. The trim controls are easily reached by the right hand, and each one works in the natural direction of the control. Perhaps the biggest bonus of all is the excellent cockpit view both of outside and inside. It may sound odd to praise an aeroplane for this latter quality but it is an important aspect, particularly when a lot of instrument flying is done. The Blenheim's instruments, apart from the standard blind-flying panel, are not so much grouped in the cockpit as thrown together haphazardly. But somebody has studied the placing of the ancillary instruments and controls in the Beau, so that the engine dials are to-gether and easily checked, minor gauges not so frequently required are a little out of the way but still visible when wanted and close by their appropriate controls when appropriate.

The Blenheim cockpit has a multitude of small windows separated by metal framework like a greenhouse. These panels have a disconcerting tendency at night to pick up reflections from the cockpit lighting, so that the eye is constantly distracted by lights seemingly coming from outside the aircraft. The Beaufighter's windshield, which suffered from a similar disadvantage in its early version, is now one large perspex moulding surrounding a bullet-proof centre portion. There are few metal members to block the view, and clear-vision panels at each side and overhead can be opened to give draught-free access to the outside. Cockpit lighting is good (without being as good as later forms of ultra-violet lighting which made life easier when the Mosquito came along).

The aircraft has a good turn of speed—more than 300mph—but is heavy and not particularly manoeuvrable, a quality which it does not necessarily need for night fighting. Its worst point, from both the pilot's and navigator's angle, is the lack of heating. You can see a red-hot exhaust pipe coming out of the port engine not more than 6ft away, yet the heater can only produce a small volume of hot air close by your right heel; the RO's heater merely sends a dribble of lukewarm air to dissipate among the myriad cold draughts whistling down the fuselage. The only other drawback is a certain instability in the pitching plane which manifests itself as a tendency to tighten up in a turn, so that positive forward pressure has to be applied to the control column to maintain a steady turn.

Early modifications to overcome this instability consisted of an arm with a weight, attached low down on the control column and projecting forward; centrifugal force then acted on this arm in a turn to help hold the stick forward. The cure was later found to lie in giving marked dihedral to the tailplane. Pilots are a conservative lot, however, and many preferred the original aircraft and felt that the new tailplane was a retrograde step.

Middle Wallop was a grass airfield with two runways of 1,400 and 800yd, which undulated so that their bumps would catch the unwary coming in to land. Ten tons of Beaufighter thus required a fair degree of accuracy in the approach speed. If you had 10–15mph too much on the clock as you came over the hedge, the aeroplane would then float for a hundred yards or so before touching down at 80mph, and thus use up the spare margin of distance available for stopping. Weak brakes then meant a trip through the far hedge, or an exciting ground loop. So we all quickly learned the value of precision flying and

28

brought our aircraft in to land within 1 per cent of 105mph on
the approach and 90mph over the hedge. A sharp flare-out,
from a steep power-off glide, was enough to stall the machine
onto three points at the start of the runway.

My father sent me a letter just after I had got to the squadron,
giving me just one piece of advice. 'Never forget,' he wrote,
'that there are two periods of danger in a pilot's life. The first
is when he has flown a hundred hours and thinks he knows all
there is to know about flying. The second is when he has flown
a thousand hours and *knows* he knows all there is to know.'

I never forgot that advice, nor that the pilot who gave it to
me was endowed at the same time with sufficient sense of
aggression and humour to fly over occupied Cambrai on 1
April 1917 and drop a football on the main square from his
BE 2e; on the football was written in German 'April Fool'. So
I always tried to temper care with aggression in the air, while
at the same time not taking myself too seriously.

3 February 1942
*Peter is now a flight commander of 118 Squadron; they are still at
Ibsley, which is a satellite of Middle Wallop. Yesterday Peter was over-
due from a 'Rhubarb' low-level strafing sortie. He turned up with fuel
gauges reading zero and his fuselage full of holes half an hour after hope
was rapidly fading, without his No 2, who had been shot down. They
were attacked by six ME 109s and Peter shot down one of them and
damaged two others before a burst of cannon fire went through the R/T
set just behind his head and also cut five out of six control cables. In the
reflected light of this drama I am more than ever mad at not getting to his
squadron.* [Huddled in front of the dispersal fire afterwards
Peter could not help shaking uncontrollably, so his fellow pilots
got him so drunk that he had to stay the night at the pub. This
effected a complete cure.]

Imitating day-fighter practice, I had already bought a scarf of
dazzling hue and, despite my early conversion to the steadier
ways of the nightfighter world, this practical item was, in fact,

to be worn every time I flew from that day onwards. Besides being soft on the neck, it became a sort of mascot and shared that duty with a five-shilling piece. It still nestles in the back of my wardrobe today, faded and no longer worn, but I am too attached to it to throw it away.

4 February 1942
Today we moved into the Pheasant Inn near Lopcombe Corner on the Andover–Salisbury road. It has been commandeered as a squadron mess, so that we may observe peacefully the rather different hours which night flying imposes on us. The inn has a history going back to 1737, complete with its own highwayman, one Thomas Boulter, who enjoyed four years' success before being caught and hanged at Winchester.

Tony and I made good progress in polishing our flying and interception techniques by day. He was a good operator, with first-class fluency and patter, and we got on very well together. It is worth going through the interception procedure in a certain amount of detail, for it formed the backbone of night fighting.

AI Mk IV operated on a frequency of $1\frac{1}{2}$m. As we have seen, the main deficiency of the equipment was its poor maximum range, limited as it was by the ground returns of echoes coming back from the earth directly beneath the aircraft and on the slant. The theoretical minimum range of 800ft was more usually found to be 1,000–1,200ft in service.

These restrictions were acceptable if the German bomber were flying at more than about 15,000ft, when he could be picked up at a range of 3–4 miles by a fighter flying at approximately the same height. But if he were flying at 3,000ft and the fighter descended to this height, the maximum range of the AI was only half a mile and called for greater accuracy of ground control; it also meant that there was less latitude for the radio operator in his interception technique, because a faulty or late turn could quickly lose AI contact as the range increased beyond the height of the fighter.

Ground control of nightfighter interceptions (and day fighters too, for that matter) was carried out from GCI stations (standing for Ground Controlled Interception). These stations had RDF or radar equipment operating a radar beam through an aerial system which rotated through 360° every 20sec or so, thus giving coverage all round the set.

It will be seen that a fighter could be directed so as to approach another aircraft from the side or astern, so that they were close enough for the fighter to pick up an AI contact within range of its equipment and depending on the height at which it was flying.

Meanwhile, Luftwaffe General Kammhuber was developing his own nightfighter arm along lines not dissimilar from our own. His command totalled a little more than 250 aircraft, of which rather less than 150 were operational at any one time. These aircraft nearly all relied on ground control by *Würzburg* radar to bring them to a visual sighting of their target; the exceptions were four Junkers 88s which were equipped with the first sets of *Lichtenstein* AI. These early AI aircraft were disliked by the German pilots, who preferred to fly machines without AI because they were faster by about 25mph than the *Lichtenstein* aircraft, with their clumsy external aerial arrays and unreliable AI, which did not seem to help find their targets. As usual, however, in this sort of situation one or two individual crews persevered with the black boxes so scorned by their comrades and they gradually became successful. More and more pilots became convinced of the value of *Lichtenstein* and it was soon in most Luftwaffe nightfighters. Like our own AI Mk IV, it suffered from a maximum-range limitation equal to the height of the aircraft as a result of the ground returns; it also had an extremely restricted coverage of only some 25° either side of the fore and aft axis of the aircraft in which it was installed.

As the war progressed, I was to find that aircraft of this type, more than enemy bombers, were to form one of the principal factors in shaping my thoughts and actions.

Although their AI was always behind ours during the war, German ground control was as effective as British, if not better, until it was so heavily jammed. Their *Wassermann* early-warning radar, developed by the Gema company during the war, has been estimated by experts to have been the best early-warning radar put into service by either side. Their main ground-control radar at this time was the *Würzburg* set, and its principal characteristics were unknown to British intelligence. It was desirable to know these so that we could develop effective jammers in the secret struggle which was evolving in the radar and radio countermeasures field.

Accordingly what has been described since as the best British commando-style raid of the war was mounted on the night of 27 February 1942. A small force of paratroops and an RAF special signals NCO were airlifted from Thruxton airfield, not ten miles from where we were at Middle Wallop, and dropped on a *Würzburg* installation on the cliff tops at Bruneval in France. They took the Germans by surprise and dismantled the equipment, bringing its vitals back to England in Royal Navy assault boats.

German nightfighter control from the ground differed from our own in that each station comprised an early warner (the *Freya*) and two *Würzburgs*, one to monitor the bomber and the other to control the fighter. The information from these two sources was filtered on the spot and plotted on a special table (the *Seeburg* plotter) from which the controller directed his interception. Thus all the necessary information for a situation was available in one place which could, however, only deal with one bomber and one fighter at a time. Each zone so covered was overlapped on either side by another. The four elements of this complex gave rise to the name 'four-poster bed' which, in German, is *Himmelbett* or, literally translated, 'bed of heavenly bliss'.

The chain of these stations stretched down the Dutch coast and on into Belgium and France, and became known in the RAF as the Kammhuber line. It was adequate to combat

Page 33 Self and Tony Nordberg dressed up for an altitude climb at 54 OTU in December 1941. The Blenheim Mk IV was unheated, and managed to stagger to 23,500ft

Page 34 Self as a pilot officer with 604 Squadron, outside the Pheasant Inn near Salisbury in 1942

Bomber Command's prevailing tactics of raiding on a broad front and stretched over a period of time; later techniques of concentration in time and space swamped the system, and new methods had to be evolved (which the Germans proved themselves capable of doing at short notice).

Although great strides had been made in this country in AI and GCI since the beginning of the war, there were still plenty of faults and interceptions were far from straightforward exercises without hitches. But the early bugs had been largely ironed out by the pioneers and, by 1942, it was just a question of practice and serviceability.

One of the teams which had done a great deal to bring AI technique to such perfection as it now enjoyed was John Cunningham and his radio operator Jimmy Rawnsley, both auxiliaries from 604's peacetime days at Hendon. Cunningham's almost uncanny perfection and accuracy in flying, coupled with a calmness under any conditions of weather or aircraft behaviour, so that his high technical skill could be brought to bear on an interception even under the most arduous circumstances, were already of legendary proportions by this time. These were the qualities which made him such an excellent chief test pilot for de Havilland's after the war.

Not quite so well known outside his own circle, perhaps, was Jimmy Rawnsley. At thirty-eight he was fourteen years older than his pilot and well above the average age even for 604, which still had a proportion of pre-war auxiliaries, most of whom were rather more than the usual age for operational aircrew (Tony and I were two of the second generation aircrew only just beginning to arrive at the squadron as replacements, and we were about twenty years old). In contrast with his pilot's almost baby face, fair wavy hair and startlingly blue eyes, Jimmy was just over 5ft 3in, cherubic of countenance with ruddy cheeks rather like a goblin, with a volatile (and suitably impish) sense of humour. He had a becoming modesty, for on his left breast he wore the ribbons of the DFC and the DFM and bar—and he was to earn the DSO before the end of the

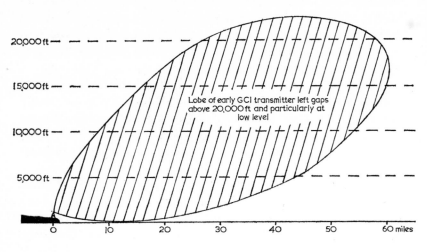

Lobe of early GCI transmitter left gaps above 20,000 ft and particularly at low level

25,000 ft
20,000 ft
15,000 ft
10,000 ft
5,000 ft

0   10   20   30   40   50   60 miles

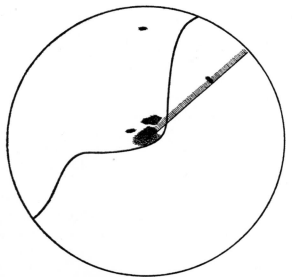

GCI aerial rotated through 360°. PPI (plan position indicator) produced 'blip' as transmitter 'illuminated' target. Coastline was painted on the tube face. Town on headland shows permanent echoes where targets cannot be seen. There are two aircraft on this tube: one due north at about 40 miles from GCI, the other north east at about 30 miles. Heights were obtained from a separate tube and friendly aircraft could enlarge their own echo by means of an IFF set (Identification Friend or Foe)

echoes. To concentrate the beam in this way required a reflector behind the transmitting aerial. Questions of manageability required the aerial to be fairly small or the reflecting dish would not fit into the nose of an aeroplane, but the aerial had to half the wavelength of the radar it was serving so this, in turn, meant that a reduction in wavelength had to be achieved. Not until a suitable valve was developed, however, could enough power be transmitted on the lower wavelength under consideration (10cm) to give workable results. The magnetron valve had been developed and a 10cm AI had been flying for exactly a year at this time; we were shortly to get some of the early production sets to help us find these elusive low fliers. But more of that later.

20 March 1942
Peter invites me to a party at Ibsley and I fly down for the night. The thrash is given by the film crew and cast who have been making The First of the Few *on location with 118 Squadron for the past few weeks. The stars are Leslie Howard, David Niven and the Spitfire (and Peter H-W with his fellow pilots). They put on a wizard do which lasts until the small hours.*

Given a certain level of competence, the human problem of flying an aeroplane at night (or in conditions of no visibility by day) is largely one of confidence. A pilot without confidence spends too much of his time staring fixedly at his instruments and is not able to relax. Tenseness causes his senses to tell him that his aircraft is acting strangely and he has to concentrate all the more on the true state of affairs as revealed by his instruments, until he has to exert positive will-power to believe the latter instead of his sensations. Only by practice and experience can a pilot reach a state at which he can relax sufficiently to look upon the physical control of his aircraft as incidental to the job in hand, so that he can get on with other problems while automatically ensuring that he obeys the orders of the ground controller or his own radio operator.

We had one pilot in the squadron who took off one dark night with the clear-vision panel over his head inadvertently left open. This, as might be expected, caused a roar of air which hammered and buffeted the canopy, but the pilot was so tense that he never noticed the noise for the entire three-hour trip.

John Cunningham's object in taking up all new pilots was to show them that a Beaufighter was nothing to be frightened of. Many new aircraft which enter service are the subject of alarmist rumours. They are either flying coffins, uncontrollable in a spin, won't fly on one engine or make the pilot sterile through high-frequency vibrations (this latter also went for AI in general and 10cm AI in particular when it first came in). In fact, apart from its slight fore-and-aft instability, the Beaufighter was one of the nicest aircraft to fly ever built, and a demonstration of precision flying by the CO was the surest way of instilling confidence in inexperienced pilots.

21 March 1942
A Martin Marauder of the US Army Air Force comes over the airfield at lunchtime under low cloud, obviously lost. He makes a couple of rapid circuits, somehow missing Danebury Hill, and then has a stab at it. Our long runway is only 1,400yd of grass and, whether the Yank is used to double that, whether he forgets to put down his flaps, or whether he just leaves the throttles wide open, it is quite obvious even to him that he isn't going to stop inside the hedge unless he does something. He pulls up the undercart when he's half way down the runway and still going strong; that does the trick—just. He steps out of the resulting mess and we carry him off to the bar. This is a golden opportunity to sing our version of 'John Brown's Body', and we don't miss it.

> *We're flying Flying Fortresses at 30,000 feet.*
> *We're flying Flying Fortresses at 30,000 feet.*
> *We've bags of point five ammo and a teeny weeny bomb,*
> *And we drop the bastard from so high we don't know where it's gone.*

> *Glory, glory, shall we drop it?*

Duckett, take-off into the murk; Per Bugge, one of our Norwegians, is then brought to readiness and he also goes off. All three have brief sightings of Heinkels in the opaque haze but, although the CO and Crew both exchange shots with their bombers, nothing definite occurs. JC is also intercepted by a 600 Squadron aircraft, who fortunately recognises him as friendly in the difficult light. Both Rawnsley and Duckett report interference of varying intensity on the AI, which took the form of scattered 'noise' traces, or 'grass', on the CRT, becoming worse as they flew south towards France. This is evidently some form of enemy jamming. We had the last laugh, however, because some Spitfires in the better weather down in Cornwall took off and went and beat up the Luftwaffe's radio-beam transmitter so, not only was there a high proportion of interceptions in dicey weather, despite their attempts at jamming, but also the Heinkels were not able to find their way home by their beam afterwards.

There were rumours about now that we were to be visited by a team of psychiatrists. Whether they thought we were odd people or needed more carrots (this was, of course, a fallacy based on a half truth about vitamins, as was the legend about John's eyesight being catlike, which gave rise to so much annoyance in the squadron), I cannot say. At all events, we were determined not to disappoint them and had a script ready for when they arrived. One of us was briefed to twitch visibly, another to wear dark glasses all the time and yet another to shout, 'Turn that damn radio off! Can't you see it's getting on my nerves!' Books were to be thrown, raw carrots to be chewed nervously and people were to jump visibly whenever anybody addressed them. We were sorry when the visit was unaccountably cancelled.

23 and 24 April 1942
About fifty German aircraft raid Exeter each night. B Flight is on for the second of these two raids and Tony and I are duly ordered off in our turn. Our AI is immediately found to be u/s [unserviceable] *and we return and stand over the special signals mechs as they struggle to find the fault. We go off again but it is still no good. This time we ask to stay up and try cat's-eye interceptions without AI and with the aid of search-*

43

lights, but we have no luck. Cunningham has a visual of a DO 215 but is not able to bring it to combat.

24–27 April 1942
Bomber Command raids Rostock on four consecutive nights, mounting a total of nearly 500 sorties.

25 April 1942
Two waves of about seventy-five German aircraft raid Bath. Tony and I are relegated to an inland GCI and don't even have a chase. Stanley Skinner destroys a DO 215. Examination of the bodies in the wreckage reveals that the aircraft was carrying one more crew member than usual. Charlie Birch (our Intelligence Officer) tells us that the extra man was one of the German squadron's cooks, along for the ride. Whether he says this to foster his reputation for knowing all about the enemy, or because he really does know it for a fact, we find hard to decide. He speaks with confidence, however, and we are finally convinced.

The Bomber Command raids stung Hitler to a frenzy and he vowed vengeance, hence the raids on Exeter and Bath. On 26 April Hitler promised to flatten all British cities of architectural beauty (he had, in fact, already issued a signal on 14 April ordering a resumption of bombing on England and he was now working on the assumption that these targets would be lightly defended in the absence of munitions factories) and said that he would amend his copy of Baedeker's guide as each city was destroyed. The attacks were promptly christened the Baedeker raids by the British press. There followed attacks on the cathedral cities of Norwich, York and Canterbury but heavy losses, particularly among training personnel, who were pressed into service to swell the numbers, compelled the Luftwaffe to call off these reprisals in the summer. As an example of losses, crews of KG.2 (Kampfgeschwader No 2—Bomber Group 2) comprising normally 100–120 aircraft, were reduced from just under a hundred in January 1942 to a quarter of that number by September of the same year.

To supplement these night attacks, the Germans sometimes sent over single aircraft by day, when cloud cover was sufficient to afford protection from the waiting Spitfires. It was just such an occasion as this when the squadron had three visuals on 4 April. These rather specialised raids were carried out by KG.100, recalled from the Russian front and put back on to their original role of beam-flying pathfinders. They were equipped with *X-Gerät*, which was a modified form of the Lorenz blind-landing system, so that they could fly along a narrow radio beam and release their bombs at a pre-arranged signal from the ground. The release point was worked out by an early form of computer carried in the aircraft, and British countermeasures consisted of blocking the computer by flooding it with signals.

As we have seen, under these weather conditions the night-fighters were usually ordered to take over day readiness from the Spitfires. There were two reasons for this. First we had AI and so could find the bombers in the thick cloud. Secondly, nightfighters had much better aids to navigation (we had a radar beacon which could be picked up on AI Mk IV using the 1½m waveband and, if it were sited along the line of the main runway, even used as a primitive form of landing beacon) and were perforce in much better instrument-flying practice; they could therefore spare more attention for the interception, without having all their efforts concentrated on the physical mastery of the elements. As soon as I was considered sufficiently experienced to take part in this day readiness, which demanded a high standard of flying when the weather was really bad with low cloud and heavy icing, I quickly got into the habit of telephoning brother Peter at Ibsley to pull his leg about not being good enough or brave enough to take on the readiness himself with his Spitfires.

45

3 A DUCKING

1 May 1942

Tony and I practise interceptions with William Hoy and Ronnie Dalton flying as a fast target. It is a fine, quiet night, as we fly at 15,000ft under Sopley control about twenty miles south of the Isle of Wight. We take it in turns to act as target and fighter.

We are cruising at +3lb of boost with 2,650rpm to give William the fast target he wants. Everything is so calm that it is almost monotonous and I start day dreaming; I think about the almost incredible system of night fighting William was on not so long ago. He flew slow old Handley Page Harrows across the path of the enemy bomber stream while someone threw aerial mines out of the back. These were suspended by long wires from parachutes, and the idea was that the Germans would fly into them and so bring themselves down. Called the Long Aerial Mine, it was codenamed 'Mutton' after its initials, and is now just about as dead.

Suddenly I am awakened from my reverie by a roughness in the starboard engine. It continues for a few seconds and then loses all power. I glance quickly at the instruments. The rpm have gone off the clock and the oil pressure is zero. I throttle back the good engine to zero boost and set the rpm to 2,400. I then try to feather the starboard engine but nothing happens.

'Hello Starlight, this is Fearsome 37 calling. I have had an engine failure and may not be able to maintain height. Over.'

'Hello 37, Starlight here. Vector three three zero for the nearest airfield, over.'

'37 OK. Standby. Out.'

I try the feathering button again, exercise the throttle and watch my airspeed carefully. This drops from its original 250mph to 220, 200,

*180 and then lower still. I realise that, if I let it go much lower, I won't
be able to hold the aircraft against the asymmetric power of the live
engine, because there won't be enough airflow passing over the rudder to
hold her straight. Meanwhile I increase power on the port engine to +3lb
boost and 2,650rpm.*

*The speed continues to fall. When it gets down to 145mph I lower
the nose slightly and start losing height, letting the speed build up to
150mph again. We are obviously not going to make it.*

*'Doesn't look too good Tony. We shall have to bale out. Switch the
IFF* [Identification Friend or Foe. A means of showing identifi-
cation by enlargement of the echo on the cathode-ray tubes of
GCI and AI sets; it also has a distress setting] *to distress.'*

*'Standing by. I'm just behind you.' His continued calmness works
wonders for me. He has already come forward to open the hatch ready for
me, and has plugged in to the spare R/T jack, just behind my seat. We
have practised this on dry land several times, much to the tolerant amusement of the rest of the squadron, aircrew and airmen alike. He taps me
smartly on the shoulder and I look round to find that he has gone.*

*I throttle back the port engine, collapse the seat and start to pull myself
backwards out of it. The next thing I remember is falling gently, suspended beneath my parachute. The moonlit sky stretches over my head like
the vault of some vast cathedral. I think I hear a splash so call out to
Tony once and then realise that it was probably the aircraft; even if it is
Tony, he won't hear me now that he's in the water.*

*The sea comes up quickly. When about to enter it I turn the release
box on my parachute harness and rap it smartly. But not smartly enough
and it is still on me as I go under. I panic because I go a hell of a way
down and so I start swimming upwards. The night air is heaven as I
break surface, but then the air bottle on my Mae West lifejacket doesn't
work, so I panic again as I wonder whether I can stay afloat. I lie on my
back and discover that the kapok in my Mae West is keeping me up but
that I am entangled in the shrouds of my parachute; fear rises again but
dies down as I struggle to break free, when I have time to start worrying
again. The sight of my dinghy pack floating on its dog lead alongside me
galvanises me into action again and I unpack the precious craft.*

The water is calm but very cold. My dinghy doesn't appear to have any leaks and my Mae West kept me up by its kapok despite the failure of the air bottle. I could be worse off. I pick up my bearings from the Pole Star and wonder how Tony is getting on.

I find myself praying frantically, realise that I am whining, so give myself a metaphorical kick in the pants and some firm instructions to make an effort to save myself. I start paddling for the shore.

Shortly afterwards the roar of a high-powered launch makes itself heard in the cold stillness.

It stops two hundred yards away and starts sweeping with its light. Joy, which had surged up within me, turns to bitter disappointment when I realise that they haven't seen me. I paddle into a position so that I am in the path of the moon's reflection on the water, and shout again and again. The noise of the powerful motors ticking over obviously drowns my voice, for the launch moves off the other way to stop once more about half a mile off. Clutching at any straw, I paddle frantically forward again but, before I have gone twenty yards, the noise of the motors tells me without looking over my shoulder that the launch is moving off once more.

So I turn towards the land again where I can just make out white cliffs and where searchlights are still playing. An aeroplane comes over and drops flares. I start swearing, under my breath at first but then out loud.

'Blast the bloody launch and those sodding flares. I'll damn well row home by myself. I don't need any help. Go on, drop your bloody flares and see if I care. I'm buggered if I'm going to row towards them.'

Whenever I stop paddling I start to shiver uncontrollably with the cold. So I go on paddling even though it feels as though my arms will drop off. I just have to keep warm.

And thus passes an hour. Two. Three. And still I paddle, for to stop makes me shake all over. I have no hope now of being picked up before dawn, but I was born in the Isle of Wight and reckon I can get ashore myself. Then I see a ship. She looks like a small trawler and is going backwards and forwards some way away, obviously looking for us.

'Ahoy! Ahoy!' I forget about the cold and my resolutions about getting myself ashore as I start shouting again.

'Ahoy!'

48

Page 51 (above) Brother Peter as a flight commander of 118 Squadron, beside his Spitfire after combat in February 1942; *(below)* Messerschmitt 110 equipped with *Lichtenstein* (small aerials) and *SN2* (large aerials)

Page 52 (above) What is now the public bar at the Pheasant Inn near Salisbury. In 1942 it was 604 Squadron's Officers' Mess. From left to right: Micky Phillips, John Cunningham, the author, Johan Råd, Bob Wright and Per Bugge; *(below)* the Beaufighter Mk VI in which Mac and I shot down a Heinkel 111 while it was carrying a flying bomb (FZG 76). The thimble nose is the plastic dome covering the scanner of AI Mk VIII

dinghies on the night of 1 May, but nobody would believe that they could see such a small target!

My brother was promoted to squadron leader and sent on rest to command a communications flight at Colerne. This was near to my aunt's house just outside Bath, where my mother was living for the duration, and looked as though it could come in useful for getting home on leave.

23 May 1942

Today John Cunningham and Jimmy Rawnsley are ordered off in thick cloud to investigate a bogey approaching the coast in daylight. They get an AI contact and there follows a chase in and out of cloud as far as Shaftesbury, with Cunningham getting to visual range on a Heinkel 111. There is no horizon, only an all-pervading blinding whiteness where, despite a filtered light from the sun, visibility is reduced to about a thousand yards, interspersed with darker patches where rainstorms cut this to 300yd or less. The Heinkel is a match for Cunningham, for he turns into the attack each time, and twists like a master under these difficult conditions so that Jimmy has to bring the CO back to visual range by AI on three occasions. The sightings are so brief and the German's actions so vigorous that no shots can be exchanged as the two aircraft flash past each other, turning hard.

Finally, the winding match tightens so much and the dive is so steep that the CO reckons he is nearly on his back and fast running out of altitude. The artificial horizon had long since toppled, the ASI [Air Speed Indicator] is showing the incredible speed of 380mph and the altimetre is unwinding fast. Cunningham breaks off the engagement and sets about re-establishing equilibrium on primary instruments. At that moment the Heinkel flashes past again, showing its plan view and seemingly going straight down. AI contact is lost and Sopley can give no more help.

Back at the airfield we hear before the CO lands that an HE 111 has crashed near Cranbourne Chase, having failed by a small margin to pull out before hitting high ground. JC is quite rightly credited with its destruction, although he had not fired a shot. We learn later from intelligence that the German pilot was none other than the commanding officer of the development unit of KG.100, our beam-bombing pathfinder friends.

The station commander receives a letter from Salisbury Council today, complaining that a bomb was dropped on the city last week. What is the point, they say, of having a nightfighter squadron at hand if the Luftwaffe can drop a bomb on the place? One bomb, mark you, not two or twenty-two. A diplomatic reply is sent.

30 May 1942
Bomber Command raid Cologne with the incredible total of more than one thousand aircraft.

Some idiot at Air Ministry with nothing better to do, has decreed that NCO aircrew must call officers of the same crew 'sir', even in the air. Tony and I have a good laugh at this (the letter doesn't say what he should call me when we are both paddling dinghies in the Channel); the writer of the order has obviously never experienced the comradeship of a flying crew, probably hasn't flown in his life. Gonsalves, earthy as ever, passes a comment which is unprintable.

Radio countermeasures were beginning to become fashionable and jamming was becoming a popular pastime. People were obviously worried about the effects of various forms of jamming if used by the Germans against us, and one of the toys we were given to play with was a device which went by the code name of *Beechnut*. This was a means of communicating with aircraft in the event of R/T being effectively jammed. It looked rather like a fruit machine or 'one-armed bandit'. There were three drums, each with about a dozen different instructions on it, and the ground controller could trigger the three desired instructions to the pilot of his choice by means of a radio transmission on a wavelength hard to jam. We tried the equipment out for two weeks and then it disappeared as mysteriously as it had materialised.

13 June 1942
We have now received a new AI. It operates in the 10cm waveband and

directs its pulses from a small aerial backed by a reflecting dish, which serves to concentrate the power into a narrow beam directed straight forward from the nose of the aircraft. The effect of this is to avoid sending any pulses downwards, so that there is no direct ground return. We can thus see farther than our height. This is AI Mk VII and it produces a coverage rather like the shape of an egg pushed along in front of the aircraft. Tony and I fly with it for the first time today (Tony having spent some time on the ground trainer which has been with us for a few days now), and we find that we are getting three and four miles at 5,000ft over the land and as much as five or six miles over the sea.

20 June 1942
Johan Råd shows us how bats have quite efficient rear warning AI. As they dive and swoop in the dusk, he throws a stone so that it is falling straight down behind the bat as it passes. The creature's operator immediately thinks he has a contact on a possible prey astern and orders a peel-off and follow. The bat dives after the stone, realises that the target has been swallowed up in the ground returns and that it is reaching the same sort of situation which JC had with his Heinkel last month, and breaks off the chase. We do it again and again, and it works every time.

15 June 1942
Tony and I fly a canopy exercise for Hurn searchlights. This comprises flying across the airfield at about 1,000ft until the searchlights latch on to you, and then twisting and turning to try and shake them off. The inside of the cockpit is brilliantly lit by the combined effects of about twenty searchlights and it is important for the pilot to keep his head well down with his eyes on his instruments, for he will be temporarily blinded if he looks outside. We make about four runs and then I decide that I will really shake them off, so I dive and twist until they do, in fact, lose us and go out. That teaches them. I have been half watching outside the cockpit to see how the lights are getting on and now I look inside again. Christ! The altimeter shows only 200ft and the airfield is about that height above datum. I pull the nose up sharply and start climbing, muttering something to Tony.

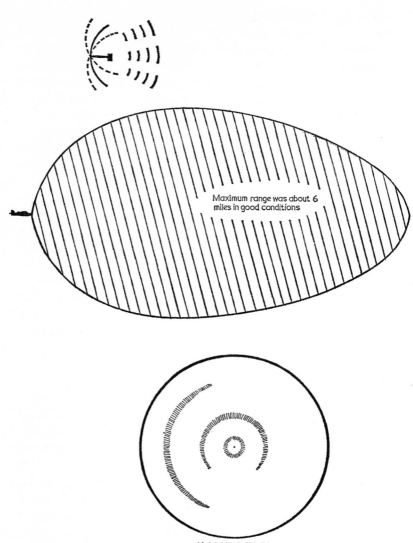

Maximum range was about 6 miles in good conditions

AI Mk VIII DISPLAY

A single tube gave both range and angle off simultaneously. This shows two target echoes : one well to port and level at about four miles, and the other dead ahead and slightly up at closer range. The centre ring is the direct pulse return as soon as the Hurricane pilot started fidgeting. In bad weather the single-seater suffered from not having blind-landing equipment, so that it was in trouble if it lost its Havoc. But by far the most telling argument was that, having got to a position from which the Havoc could aim itself and illuminate its target, it seems almost beyond belief that anybody, let alone the wartime Prime Minister, could imagine that it wouldn't be better to aim cannon shells rather than a searchlight. If the Havoc could hit the bomber with a light, surely it could dispense with the staggering weight and expense of batteries and hit it with four cannons; this would also dispense with a Hurricane. There could also, of course, be occasions when the Turbinlite illuminated the bomber correctly but the Hurricane failed to shoot it down.

Ten of these flights were scattered up and down the country, wasting manpower and machines. They were always kept out of the way if any trade came over, while preference was given to the Beaufighters, and theirs must have been a frustrating life. In fact, the only aircraft they ever shot down turned out to be one of our own four-engined Short Stirlings, whose crew bailed out and were stupidly brought to the same airfield as the errant Turbinlite flight; there was nearly a riot. They were all disbanded before 1943 was over but, as late as September 1942, a Turbinlite Mosquito with its own guns was considered. Three unarmed versions were building at the time and it took a scathing report from John Cunningham, while he was commanding 85 Squadron early in 1943, finally to kill the project.

6 August 1942
For some time now the squadron has been flying nightly to Predannack on the tip of the heel of Cornwall with an AI Mk VII Beau. We fly patrols against the early-morning low-flying minelayers—the 'milk train'— hoping that our better AI will get more results than the resident squadron's Mk IV equipment. Tony and I go tonight and the trip is uneventful.

Trade in general was slack at this time. The Luftwaffe did a bit of minelaying at night and mounted raids on the odd town such as Newcastle, Sunderland or Birmingham. Their bomber force was low in aircrew, because they had not foreseen a long war and their training organisation was inadequate to replace anything more than slow wastage. The Battle of Britain and the invasion of Russia had used up their large reserve pool, and improved British night fighting was now causing losses too great to be easily replaced. On 17 August the United States gave notice of things to come with its first daylight raid on France.

The Germans showed in this month, however, that they were not to be outdone in the matter of radio countermeasures. Since 8 March our bombers had been using a new grid-system navigation aid called *Gee*. On 4 August this was jammed for the first time, and crews reported that it was unusable over Germany.

1 November 1942
To Predannack again. We have to land at Exeter and, on take-off at dusk under their sector control, we are vectored on our way. After climbing on course for about five minutes Tony gets a contact dead ahead and slightly above, closing fast. Then another and another. I look up and there, about 1,000ft above us and half a mile ahead, I can just make out in the gathering darkness the Exeter barrage balloons. Fat and menacing, they are silhouetted against the afterglow. I turn smartly onto a reciprocal course and bark into the R/T.

'Who's the silly bastard who nearly had us through our own balloons?'

There is much confusion and apology from below, for they were in direct close control of our flight, but I am angry and frightened until we are nearly at Predannack.

On patrol that night we are heavily shot up by the convoy we are supposed to be protecting. That teaches me not to get too close.

Our patrol is after the milk train. This is the pre-dawn sortie often put out by the Luftwaffe to lay mines in our area. It is uneventful and we set course for Middle Wallop after we have been stooging up and down, up and down, 090°–270°, 090°–270°, for an hour and a half.

The first fingers of dawn are just beginning to etch the eastern sky ahead of us as we start on the hour's flight homewards.

By the time we reach base, the sun is well up and spilling daylight into the sleepy valleys beneath us. Tony and I are cold and tired, but tired with the feeling of a job properly done. We have been protecting those homes down there. Ahead looms the spire of Salisbury Cathedral, pricking through a light layer of early morning mist; a train puffs its way from somewhere to somewhere, leaving a trail of cotton wool behind it.

'Let's see if they're awake at the Pheasant,' I suggest, and there is a grunt of approval from the back; it's too cold to talk much.

I dive the aircraft until we are doing about 260mph as we come down from 1,500ft to under 200ft. Along the Salisbury–Andover road ahead I can see the Pheasant outlined dimly in the mist. Lower we go until we flash overhead with what I know is an unheralded roar, for the Beau's approach under these circumstances is completely silent. I pull up, call flying control at base and enter the circuit. Beating up the mess is not exactly approved, but one pass every now and then is tolerated; we don't make a habit of it and we don't do it more than once each time. It will be our turn soon to be almost shaken out of bed by some other pilot, full of the thought that everyone ought to be up and about, to enjoy the promise of a fine day.

4   LUFTWAFFE TACTICS

7 December 1942

The squadron is posted to Predannack. It is the obvious move, but we have been hoping against hope that at least it wouldn't happen until after Christmas, for we like our life. Tony drives my car down for me and I fly the squadron intelligence officer. We go in an enormous formation of seventeen aircraft and arrive over Predannack with a certain amount of panache. We are a good squadron and we know it; we want our new station to know it too.

We join the circuit and follow close upon each other's heels, too close for the comfort of flying control, who tell us so. We say that we are OK, particularly as there is a stiff breeze blowing straight down the runway. As the first aircraft is touching down, the second is on final approach and the third is across wind. The runway caravan fires a red signal flare at No 2 to tell him that he is too close and to go round again. It is ignored and we stream in to perfect landings close behind each other. As I land I pull the flaps up and open the throttle to make room for the man behind me, and we have five aircraft on the runway at once: one turning off at the far end, one getting near him, one in the middle with throttles half open to keep rolling, one pulling up his flaps having just settled and one touching down. It is an exhibition of precision flying but we are lucky nothing goes wrong, for we are disobeying distinct orders from the ground, who run out of red cartridges trying to stop us showing off.

Predannack was on the top of the cliffs at the tip of Cornwall and was the first bit of land seen by shattered aircraft limping back from the Bay of Biscay, so we used to collect a lot of shot-up Coastal Command aircraft. There was almost always a strong wind blowing and plenty of rain made sure that the ground off the tarmac was nearly all bog. Our dispersal was a collection of Nissen huts, which was a change from the central heating of Middle Wallop. They were constantly dirty because people entering could hardly avoid bringing a good deal of mud with them. The only bright spot was the Officers' Mess; this was the Polurrian Hotel down in Mullion Cove and was warm and comfortable.

Left to our own resources a good deal as regards amusement, card playing came into its own both on and off duty. We also went for walks over the fine moorlands and several of us did some shooting. It was the Norwegians who first discovered the bevy of WAAF beauties at Treleaver GCI and it was our natural duty to liaise with our local control station. A Mrs Hammond had a cottage nearby and was a most generous hostess. She seemed to look upon entertaining the RAF as her war work, and she did it very well. The first time I went there I entered her door a complete stranger, had a glass of punch thrust into my hand and then proceeded to enjoy myself more than I had ever done before at a party of people unknown to me.

Tony and Rosemary rented a small bungalow near to the mess and they were very good to the whole squadron. When we had been out pub crawling or to Mrs Hammond's we would descend on their house and eat up all that was left in the larder. We were even known to wake them up when they had not been drinking with us, by singing 'Oh, Oh, Antonio' outside their bedroom window; instead of throwing a bucket of water over us, Rosemary cooked us all bacon and eggs.

9 December 1942

Jimmy Lomas and I fly a low-level sector recce round the coastline in loose formation, taking it in turns to lead. The official object is to get to know the local landmarks so we shall recognise the countryside; in fact it is an excuse for a bit of low flying. We get lower and lower until we are below the top of the cliffs in places. On landing back I twit Jimmy about flying beneath the power cable joining some lighthouse to the shore.

'Power cable?' says Jimmy, 'I didn't see any cable.'

63

I had, and I had climbed over it rather than follow him underneath.

At this time the scientists were worried about German night interception techniques. They were still uncertain whether *Emil Emil* was airborne radar or infra red, but they thought that it was a radar operating just below 500 megacycles per second (AI Mk IV was 200mc/s). On 3 August a Wellington of 1473 Wireless Investigation Flight (later 192 Squadron) at Gransden Lodge took off on one of their regular 'ferret' flights to listen to the waveband around that figure. They were to fly so as to invite interception and then, to make sure that it was a night-fighter they were hearing, they were to allow the enemy aircraft to close in to visual range, searching the spectrum for his radar transmissions. The exact wavelength was then to be coded and wirelessed back to England as soon as it was positively identified (they weren't given a very high survival chance, it will be noted; this was a virtual suicide mission).

Distinct radar transmissions on 490mc/s were identified and a JU 88 duly attacked the Wellington. Heavily shot up, with four out of six of the crew badly wounded, the aircraft reached England on half an engine and ditched near the coast at dawn; all the crew were rescued (and later decorated).

While this was going on, the finishing touches were being put to the installation of the first AI Mk IX in a Beaufighter of TFU at Defford aerodrome. TFU was the Telecommunications Flying Unit, and was the flying part of TRE which, it will be remembered, had been moved earlier in the year to Malvern. Mark IX was a 10cm AI, employing a narrow spiral scanner rather like Mk VII and VIII but with the refinement that it could be 'locked on' to any target selected by the radio operator. Its first flight showed that it was liable to lock on to *Window*—the tinfoil strips dropped by aircraft to swamp enemy radar by giving a multitude of false blips. The AI was modified and, two days before Christmas, the equipment was on its second trip, under the control of its designer, when both it and its target aircraft dropping the *Window* were attacked by a Spitfire. The Beaufighter with the precious AI Mk IX was shot down and the pilot and scientist were both killed; the target aircraft was badly damaged but managed to land at Coltishall.

The Americans, who had been given the results of all our early work on radar together with the lines on which we were working, had developed a 10cm AI of their own which proved superior to our lock follow equipment. This was their SCR 720 (Signals Corps Radio 720), which we designated AI Mk X. It used a fully rotating scanner which could also nod up and down through segments of the sky which could be selected by the RO. The resulting display was a form of PPI showing a plan view of the radar search in front of the fighter, with a second CRT giving relative height. AI Mk X was to become standard equipment in nearly all British and American nightfighter squadrons.

This type of radar was advancing by leaps and bounds at this stage. As I said earlier, it was all made possible by the magnetron valve, an invention which it is hard to value too highly.

Had we but known it at the time, Christmas Eve saw the opening of a new era in aerial warfare. The first successful ramp launching of a flying bomb took place in Germany, and the pilotless aircraft which was to cause such disruption and damage eighteen months later began its deadly career in earnest. The V2, which arrived on the scene after the V1, had, paradoxically, started flying earlier in the year and had achieved a height of 50 miles and a speed of over 3,000mph early in October.

18 February 1943
We move to Ford. We have had no joy at all while in Cornwall and we all hope we are going to a more active sector. As we are to take over a new lot of Beaufighters, all fitted with AI Mk VII, we leave our old ones behind and fly up in a couple of ancient Harrows.

After we have landed, William Hoy, who has been on the advance party, greets us.

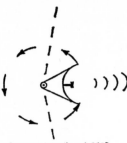

Scanner rotates through 360°
in plan but only transmits forward

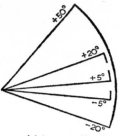

Scanner nods between one of two alternative upper
limits and one of three alternative lower limits selected
by the navigator

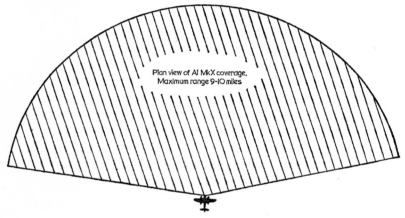

Plan view of AI MkX coverage.
Maximum range 9-10 miles

AI Mk X DISPLAY

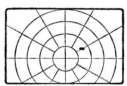

C-scope elevation display, with clock
face graticule as recommended by the
night wing of the Central Fighter
Establishment. Radar echo or 'blip'
shows a target 30° off at two o'clock.
(circles show every 20°)

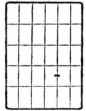

B-scope shows same target in plan view, 30°
to starboard at 3 miles on 10 mile range.
Vertical graticule lines show each 30°,60°and
90° to port and starboard. Horizontal lines
denote one or two-mile range markers depending
on selection of time base by navigator

'It's lucky you didn't arrive half an hour ago,' he says with a grin. 'A Focke-Wulf 190 went across the aerodrome at about 50ft. I should think he goes on his knees every night and prays for a Harrow, let alone two.'

At last we were back from exile and in the war again. We had instructions to be operational the night that we got there, and there was plenty of activity. The Fighter Interception Unit, of which more later, was stationed at Ford as well, and their job was to experiment with new forms of airborne radar destined for Fighter Command: AI in all its forms, IFF, rear warners and a hundred and one other pieces of equipment. They also provided two aircraft every night for the defensive programme, duly moving up and down the roster in their turn. The first night we were installed one of their Beaufighters was shot down and the crew killed. We had several scrambles that night but nothing came our way.

This sort of activity went on fairly consistently. The Germans were making short raids on London at night with bombers, and tip-and-run raids on the south coast with fighters by day. A Focke-Wulf 190 firing its guns had a particular sound and I recall sitting in a tearoom at Bognor one afternoon soon after our arrival, when this characteristic stutter could be heard coming along the front. Without hesitation I threw myself on

---

Fig 4   *AI Mk X*

In AI Mk X, both the reflecting mirror (or scanner) and the aerial rotated horizontally through a full circle at 350rpm, while a second motor caused the whole assembly to nod in elevation between angles of $+50°$ and $-20°$ to the horizontal. Within these limits, the navigator was able to select reduced elevation coverage as shown in the drawing (in order to reduce ground returns, to cut out interference from other echoes well above or below the selected target, or to increase the blip repetition rate through quicker scanning of the target).

The aerial transmitted only when the scanner pointed forward of the beam but, because the aerial was fixed to the mirror and rotated with it—as was not the case with Mk VIII—power and sensitivity of Mk X remained constant. The full range of 8–10 miles was therefore achieved out to one side as well as ahead; accuracy of D/F was constant (about 5°) at all angles off, because the beam width of 10° remained unaltered.

the floor against the wall and waited. When a motor cycle went past the door I could have wished that I was not in uniform.

21 February 1943
Cloud is down to 600ft and it has been raining all morning. The wind eddies round the dispersal hut in gusts, causing the rain to batter against the windows and swirl in through the door every time it is opened. We huddle round the stove and get the cards out; there is no flying.

The phone rings and it is Ops. Not only are we to come to day readiness but they want somebody off. It appears that there is an 'important person' visiting the Horsham area and he merits a standing patrol. Tony and I get the job of being first off and we gather our things together preparatory to making a dash through the rain to M for Mother, which is waiting faithfully on its hard standing 200yd away.

'All set, Tony?' I tuck my helmet inside my leather flying jacket so as to keep rain off the microphone, earphones and R/T plug, and I look at him without enthusiasm. Ian Joll pokes his nose round the corner of the door at this moment and offers to run us out to our aircraft in his staff car.

We don't take long over starting up but the mechanics are wet through by the time we taxi out. We take off in a flurry of spray, with water flying off the propeller tips and streaming back off the wings. Wheels up, throttle back and straight on to instruments as we are almost immediately into the low cloud scudding overhead.

We call sector operations on Channel D and are ordered due east to patrol the coast at 15,000ft. There is thick cloud all the way and it is a steady grind on instruments. On patrol we fly east for fifteen minutes, do a rate one turn through 180° to port and then fly west for fifteen minutes. Only occasional corrections from the controller serve to punctuate the silence, for Tony knows that I am in no mood for light-hearted chat.

And that's the way it stays for three monotonous hours: solid cloud, eyes on the blind-flying panel, monosyllables from Tony in the back, grunts from me in the front. It is cold. Eventually somebody else comes up to relieve us and we return to base, where conditions, thank God, haven't got any worse. We grope our way down through cloud over the sea (no hills to run into there), make a tight circuit so as not to lose sight of the aerodrome once we find it, turn over the bend of the river and slither in to a

68

*landing. By the time we reach the dispersal hut again we are both very
wet and cold.*

I hope the important person was worth it.

3 March 1943
*Blitz on London. Tony and I fly a three-hour night patrol off Beachy
Head and see nothing. After refuelling we go off again to patrol the
Kenley area; again there is no trade for us.*

The CO opened the squadron score a few nights later with a
DO 217 destroyed south of the Isle of Wight. William Hoy
claimed a HE 177 a little later, but there were doubts as to
whether the Luftwaffe was using this aircraft on operations,
despite several reported combats.

13 March 1943
*My twenty-first birthday. Peter is now on his second tour, this time with
610 Squadron at West Hampnett, about ten miles west of Ford. We land
there after our NFT and find that he shot down an FW 190 off Beachy
Head two days ago. Tony and I are on the programme tonight and our
first patrol off Worthing is shortened because the blind-flying panel be-
comes u/s. There is a raid and we are scrambled again later in another
aircraft; we get a contact which turns out to be a Whitley. I am beginning
to wonder whether we have a jinx.*

14 March 1943
*A Flight is on tonight, so Tony and Rosemary lay on a marvellous party
for me one day late. Most of B Flight is there and we keep it going into
the small hours.*

7 April 1943
*I fly the CO's aircraft on NFT. Jimmy Lomas is testing with us and he
takes-off just in front of us. The windsock is gyrating about on the end of
its mast and there is a strong cross wind; the sight of Jimmy's aircraft
drifting sideways almost before its wheels come off the ground makes me
think a bit. As I take-off the force of the wind strikes home (it is later
confirmed as gusting 50–60mph at an angle of up to 60° to the east/west
runway). I call up flying control.*

E 69

'Hello, Coachride, this is Razor 37 here. Will you ring up the flight commander of B Flight and suggest to him that he doesn't let anyone else off until he's been off himself?'

'OK 37, we'll do that.'

Ian Joll takes one look outside the door and cancels all further flying. Jimmy and I finish our NFTs and return. I have a look at the windsock and it is still across the runway in use. This time it looks to me as though it is anything up to 90° off and so I speak to flying control.

'Hello, Coachride. This is Razor 37. Are you still using the east/west runway, or have you gone over to the south/north?'

'No 37. Come in on the east/west. The wind is high and gusting, but you will be better off on that runway.'

'OK. Here goes.' And with that I make my approach. As I touch down, crabbing sideways down the runway, I feel the starboard wing being lifted by the wind. It goes up and up as I juggle frantically with the controls and throttles, until I think we are going over onto our backs. We finally get back onto three wheels, but by now 4ft of my port wing tip is bent up at right angles where it has scraped the ground.

'Now see what your bloody silly runway has done,' I say, for I am very angry, more with myself for letting it happen than anything else. Jimmy Lomas comes in on the grass across the runways and into wind.

I go to dispersal and apologise to the flight commander and then ring up the CO to tell him that I have broken his aeroplane.

'Yes, I know,' he replies. *'I watched it happen.'*

I then get on to flying control and fume down the mouthpiece at the flying control officer. If I had had my way I should not have broken that aeroplane.

Shortly after this we learned that 256 Squadron, who were then re-equipping with Mosquitos, would be ready to take over from us as planned in April. We were to go to Scorton, a wartime airfield and a satellite of Catterick in Yorkshire. Our role would be the defence of Middlesbrough and Hull. We were to change aircraft yet again, taking over Beaufighters with AI Mk VIII from a squadron recently converted to Mosquitos. AI Mk VIII was basically the same as Mk VII but with facilities for beacon-homing and IFF interrogation. The equipment was also much better all round, with greater maximum range and lower minimum range (AI Mk VII had been a stopgap, rushed into service in order to give nightfighters a low-seeing AI as soon as possible, pending introduction of the more sophisticated production Mk VIII a year later).

Before we left Ford Wing Commander Wood failed to return from a night patrol. He had been put into contact with a hostile aircraft and that is the last anyone ever heard of him. His place was taken by Wing Commander Michael Maxwell, whose elder brother was station commander at Ford and who had been a successful fighter pilot in World War I. Gerald Maxwell shot down twenty-five German aircraft while serving with 56 Squadron among such famous names as Maybery, McCudden, Rhys-Davids and Ball. Michael Maxwell, his junior by some fifteen to twenty years, was destined to shoot down fifteen enemy aircraft in World War II.

We lost four more of our most experienced pilots at the same time. Micky Phillips went to FIU (the experimental unit at Ford), Bernard Thwaites to a rest and then to join John Cunningham, Edward Crew and others at 85 Squadron, Per Bugge for a short tour in the Mediterranean and then on to 85, and Johan Råd who finished up on pathfinder Mosquitos. John Selway had gone, so had Gonsalves, and William Hoy was due to leave soon. I felt that this was the break-up of the squadron as I had known it. Tony and I had still not seen a vestige of the enemy and I began to think that we never would.

We had anticipated a quiet time at Scorton, but we were mistaken. The Germans were raiding Hull and Middlesbrough often enough to keep us in a state of expectancy every night. We of B Flight, however, got to the point at which we knew that the Luftwaffe would not come over when we were on the programme; with unfailing regularity the enemy came when A Flight was at readiness. They did very well out of it and brought the flight totals nearer to each other; we at this time had forty-six destroyed and A Flight gradually crept up until they were nearing the forty mark. From our arrival my log book contains an almost monotonous succession of entries for the next two months: NFT followed by CHL. That is to say we tested our aircraft during the day and then flew an uneventful night patrol on a low-looking Chain Home station. About the only variation was a fruitless air/sea rescue search Tony and I flew for one of the A Flight crews who had been shot down during the night of 15/16 May.

11 June 1943

Fly to Coltishall with John Quinton as RO for a two-week exchange with 68 Squadron [John Quinton was to give up his life after the war to an ATC cadet by handing him his parachute and pushing him out of the door, as the aircraft they were both in crashed earthwards. He was awarded a posthumous George Cross]. *The CO is Wing Commander Max Aitken, a pre-war auxiliary from 600 Squadron and a contemporary of John Cunningham. He, too, is a successful nightfighter pilot, having shot down thirteen Huns to date. Tony hasn't come with me because Maxwell wants his operator to have the experience; Tony is flying with the wing commander while we are away.*

12 June 1943

I see my first Hun and find that they do exist! We are sent after the weather recce which the Luftwaffe sends over at nought feet every evening. We find him at dusk off the East Anglian coast by pure chance and he is a JU 88, and a fast one. We pursue him low down over the water for ten minutes and cannot close the range under 1,200yd. In desperation I fire at him until my ammunition is exhausted but only see a few hits. He shoots back but, although his tracer goes all round us (enough to start John climbing forward to hold the Beau off the deck if I am hit), we are only hit half a dozen times. Return to base very downhearted, which is made worse when I find that Max Aitken wants to claim our damaged for his squadron's total; 604 resist strongly and say that it belongs to them.

17 June 1943

Box party [funeral] *for a crew who inexplicably went straight in from about 10,000ft in a Beaufighter in broad daylight. Fortunately, I have brought my black armband with me, so I can appear properly dressed.*

Many of us kept a black armband as part of our standard kit. They were, alas, used all too often.

23 June 1943
After a dusk patrol we are ordered off again at one o'clock in the morning. We get a contact and identify it as a Beaufighter.

Apparently the 68 crew at Scorton has shot down a Hun. So both squadrons have changed their tune about our damaged JU 88 and neither wants it now!

25 June 1943
Fly back to Scorton as our two weeks are up. Far from generating friendly relations, our exchange has caused angry telephone calls as each squadron has tried to claim first our damaged JU 88 and then the other crew's DO 217 destroyed. Not a success. Tony got a DO 217 probably destroyed with the CO while we were away.

We arrive back to find Micky Phillips visiting us. He has flown up in a Mosquito from FIU at Ford and our mouths water at the sight of this magnificent aircraft. Micky says carelessly that it is rather clapped out, but we would give our eyeteeth for it (and he knows it). I ask him what it's like at FIU, as I realise that I must be coming to the end of my tour with 604 before too long. I get the gen and ask him if he will put in a good word for me if I apply to go there on rest.

Next day our best bridge player spun in. He had been threatening to do this for some time as he used to beat up dispersal regularly at nought feet, and then carry out a very tight turn. We all warned him that he would have a high-speed stall and flick roll, and this is precisely what happened. He tempted Sir Isaac once too often and, to make it worse, the diary of his navigator was found to contain several references to the folly and danger of those tight turns low down, and how the RO was sure that they would both be killed through them sooner or later. He was right.

At this period a Luftwaffe nightfighter crew defected with

their JU 88 and landed in Scotland. The aircraft was equipped with *Lichtenstein* AI (*Emil Emil* of the R/T interception) and so all its secrets were revealed. This enabled our scientists to perfect a device they were working on for homing onto the *Lichtenstein* transmissions (it will be remembered that a Wellington had bravely tempted the Luftwaffe and discovered the wavelength at great personal danger) and this equipment was fitted to Beaufighters of 141 Squadron under the command of Wing Commander Bob Braham. Only able to give direction and not range, it was called *Serrate* and was used in conjunction with AI Mk IV over enemy territory, the Beaufighters homing in the general direction by means of *Serrate* and then completing the interception on AI as soon as they came within range and got a contact. Meanwhile the Fighter Interception Unit at Ford flew the first operational defensive patrols with AI Mk X, taking over where TFU left off. TFU was at Defford and was the flying unit for the scientists at Malvern; they flew experimental equipment while it was still in the early stages of being held together with string and sealing wax. FIU took them over when the pre-production equipment was made available for operational trials. They reckoned that the best way of trying things out was to use the Germans as targets, and they were proud of having shot down the first enemy aircraft with every Mark of AI to see service so far: III, IV, V (a pilot indicator modification of the Mk IV and not popular), VII and VIII; the Mk VI was a fully pilot-operated version for use in single-seaters and never got into general service.

On the other side of the North Sea a certain Major Streib, who had been prominent in the development of German night-fighters, flew the Luftwaffe's first specialist aircraft designed for this role, the Heinkel 219, and shot down five British bombers in one night as part of the proving trials. These successes were quickly followed by others, and General Kammhuber asked for priority production of the aircraft. This was agreed but, in fact, the go-ahead had already been given to the JU 188, a special version of that jack-of-all-trades, the JU 88, so the Luftwaffe nightfighters had to be content yet again with an adaptation. In any event the nightfighter command built up by Kammhuber was disbanded, as such, later in the year and absorbed into the overall fighter defence of the Reich, both by night and by day.

12 July 1943
Blitz on Hull. I am flying with Captain Smith of the Royal Norwegian Air Force as John Quinton has been posted away and the CO wants to fly with Tony again. We are scrambled for a freelance patrol and get one contact which turns out to be . . . another Beaufighter! The old jinx is working again.

The wing commander needed a new RO now that John Quinton had left and he asked Tony whether he would fly with him on a permanent basis. I did not find out about all this until Tony's refusal had been repeated and finally reluctantly accepted, or I would have been very angry. Tony took the line that it was a compliment to his ability, and I took it that Tony's refusal was a compliment to me so, in the end, ruffled feathers were smoothed.

The countermeasures war had been continuing. We have already briefly met *Window*, the strips of metal foil, cut to half the wavelength of the radar it was designed to affect, which gave a realistic appearance on the CRT of an aircraft echo when dropped in correct quantities from the sky. It had been considered so potentially dangerous to our own radar, particularly AI Mk IV and the CH stations, both of which used fairly easily affected wavelengths, that permission for Bomber Command to use it over Germany had been withheld for nearly a year. Had Air Ministry but known it, the Germans had also discovered this device and had codenamed it *Düppel*. They, too, had been fully aware of its potential and Göring himself had ordered the report on it destroyed and no further mention ever to be made of it. At all events the definition of our radars by now had been improved with the introduction of 10cm equipment, so that the decision was taken to release *Window* for operational use. It was employed with great success on the first

75

of four fire raids on Hamburg on the night of 24 July 1943, and the German radar was swamped with thousands of spurious echoes which threw the control and reporting system into chaos. Out of 746 aircraft which reached the target only twelve were lost. This raid was followed by some 250 aircraft of the USAAF in daylight on 25 and 26 July; then Bomber Command struck again on the nights 27, 29 July and 2 August. The Luftwaffe reacted quickly to the effects of *Window*, and the system of operating freelance single-engined fighters, loosely controlled by a radio running commentary, which a certain Major Herrmann had pioneered with success over Cologne earlier in the month, was pressed into immediate large-scale use. Relying on searchlights and the fires from below to illuminate the highly concentrated bomber stream, Herrmann's *Wilde Sau* (wild boar) fighters brought hope back to the depressed German High Command. Bomber Command's losses doubled on the second and third attacks on Hamburg, but huge quantities of incendiaries were dropped and only the fourth attack on the night of 2 August was ineffective, the result of bad weather rather than the Luftwaffe. The combined effects of these six raids produced the famous firestorm which raged unchecked through the city, causing temperatures up to 1,000° C and hurricane-force winds which sucked everything and everyone into the centre of the conflagration; 50,000 people lost their lives.

14 August 1943

I decide to test the airfield guards, who always seem to me to be half asleep. I wait until dark, put on civilian clothes, take my revolver and drive to within half a mile of the aerodrome perimeter. Then, making my way on foot, I approach the Beaufighters of B Flight (which is not flying tonight) standing idle in their blast-proof dispersal bays. An airman with a rifle is strolling quite unconcernedly along the airfield boundary, silhouetted against the afterglow, and it is a simple matter to wait until he is past and then crawl under the wire fence. At one point he stops and looks round, unslinging his rifle. I suddenly realise that nobody could blame him if he took a pot at me, so I freeze, belly to the ground and my heart thumping in my throat. After a minute which lasts for an hour he moves on and I reach the nearest Beau. I remove the chocks, climb in, prime the engines and push the starter buttons. The propellers turn jerkily but the engines won't catch, so I get out again quickly, taking with me the flying helmet which I find hung on the control column. I know which aircraft will start, and seek out M for Mother, my own. As expected, she fires on both engines first time and I taxi out. A short turn round the perimeter track and then I return to dispersal, using my captured flying helmet to call up flying control and tell them that an attempt has been made to steal an aircraft. I switch off, chock the wheels, retreat the way I have come and leave the airfield in uproar behind me.

17 August 1943
Blitz on Hull. Our jinx is still working because our R/T goes u/s and Tony and I have to return. Jimmy Lomas intercepts a Wimpy [Wellington] flying towards the target just as the first bombs are falling—the third time this month that this has happened, twice to Jimmy. Our suspicions have been roused that the Germans are using one of our aircraft as a pathfinder and Jimmy asks control for permission to shoot it down. It is, of course, refused and he proceeds to find two perfectly legitimate DO 217s, one of which he destroys and the other is a probable.

Tony and I had now completed eighteen months with 604 and I knew that our time with them must be coming to an end. In Bomber Command the usual method of determining a tour of operations was by counting the number of operational trips, thirty being the usual quota. Our much safer existence, in which we were not allowed to hazard our secret equipment over enemy territory, and the higher frequency of our less dangerous operational trips (a patrol was operational and, since standing patrols were the rule for the first half of the night, a lot of ops were put in), meant that we worked up a higher total of trips, but our lives were not at risk from the enemy so much. We were, however, called upon to fly in worse weather than anybody else during the war, and this left its mark not only upon our nerves—called 'operational fatigue' by the authorities, but universally referred to by aircrew as 'the

77

twitch'—but also on our numbers. For we flew when everybody flew, and we flew when the Germans flew, and we flew when the day fighters could not fly, and we flew when nobody else flew. The bomber boys showed the greatest bravery in going back night after night to confront a steadily improving German nightfighter machine. The principal drain on our personal batteries was from grappling with Sir Isaac and his three henchmen: Turbulence, Icing and Poor Visibility. Tony and I had done ninety-seven operational patrols with 604 when we were told that we were tour expired. During all that time I had seen only one German aircraft and I felt that under these circumstances I had not completed a proper tour of operations. I had seen a bit of FIU and had heard a bit more about it from Micky Phillips, so this seemed to me a way of saving face. In some way known only to themselves, they had managed to fix it that a spell with the unit counted as a tour of operations if you came from a rest, or as a rest if you came from a tour. Not for nothing was the unit known at Fighter Command as the Operational Flying Club. I therefore applied to go to FIU with all the vigour at my command and, to my delight, I was accepted. They had no room for Tony, unfortunately, and he went on to an affiliated unit on the same aerodrome called the Navigator Radio Leaders School (radio operators had recently been rechristened navigators/radio in deference to their widening sphere of duties and also to protect them from too searching an interrogation if they fell into enemy hands, advertising by their RO brevet that they knew all about AI; as Navs/Rad they wore a simple N brevet like a lot of other aircrew). This school was established to standardise the patter and procedure of all AI operators and to help squadron navigator leaders to do their jobs better. It was a compliment to Tony that he should have been chosen for this responsible task and I was delighted that we should continue to see each other.

We both went on a week's leave and reported to our new units on the last day of August.

5 THE OPERATIONAL FLYING CLUB

My new CO was Wing Commander Roderick Chisholm (later Air Commodore R. Chisholm, OBE, DSO, DFC), an ex-604 auxiliary, and the station commander was Wing Commander Gerald Maxwell, MC, DFC, AFC, the brother of my recent squadron commander. Ford was a happy station, largely brought about by Gerald Maxwell's human approach to life. He knew the aircrews' prima donna attitudes and respected our proprietorial airs and jealously guarded privileges; he also knew how to get on with groundcrew and had a healthy disrespect for the staff unless they were really helping to keep the sharp end sharp. Rory Chisholm was an exacting and precise CO, who brought to his task of evaluating various forms of airborne radar a mathematical brain able to eschew the nonessentials. A trifle aloof, he was respected by all his aircrew but got friendship only from his senior pilots. His technical abilities as a pilot and as a semi-scientific observer were beyond question, and he drove himself as hard as, if not harder than, his men. He, too, subordinated all to the operational end and would never tolerate ground personnel interfering with any duty the flying crews had to do.

Our officers' mess at Ford was a commandeered girls' school called Tortington Hall. We liked to think that it was the origin of the story about notices beside bells on the walls of bedrooms reading: 'If anyone needs a mistress in the night, ring three times.'

The squadrons at Ford were 29, flying Mosquitos Mk XII with AI Mk VIII, and 418, a Canadian squadron, who flew

79

Mosquitos Mk VI without AI on intruder operations over enemy territory, seeking targets of opportunity.

5 September 1943

As I arrive, one Ken Davison has just been promoted to squadron leader to take over the one and only flight in FIU (which also has a peculiar post called Squadron Leader Ops. This makes room for a second squadron leader on the unit in addition to the wing commander; Chris Hartley [later Air Marshal Sir Christopher Hartley, KCB, CBE, DFC, AFC, BA] *from 604 fills this job). Ken has an incisive brain and a biting wit. He doesn't suffer fools gladly but gets on well with anybody who can pull his weight. The padré asked him this morning why he never goes to church and Ken has promised to go next Sunday if he can preach the sermon; the padré has taken him up on it.*

For the present Ken takes me out to the Mosquito to show me the tits. I have heard a lot about this aircraft and am keen to fly it. We have about half-and-half Beaufighters and Mosquitos in the flight, with a fascinating mixture of various other strange aircraft, with even more strange black boxes in them, coming and going from time to time. We climb out of the small entrance hatch and Ken tells me that I may go and get my parachute and then do a few circuits and bumps. I sign Form 700 to show that I have read the aircraft's state of serviceability, and the authorisation book to show that I understand what I am supposed to do, then I waddle out to the aircraft in front of the dispersal hut. The ground-crew help me up the flimsy collapsible metal ladder into the entrance hatch on the starboard side of the nose, and I squeeze myself through the small opening. I am a trifle nervous, and the cramped cockpit and my bulky flying clothes, Mae West and parachute make the process ungainly and sweaty. I fall back into the pilot's seat and let out a puff of breath as I grope for the unfamiliar straps. The airman helping me grunts as he pulls the shoulder straps over.

'Don't worry, sir,' he grins. 'They say a Mossie's like a virgin: difficult to get into but lovely when you're there.'

I laugh, the tension is released and my benefactor gets down and closes the door. The aircraft is a dream and I am quite at home straight away. The cockpit layout isn't as good as the Beaufighter—the left hand has to transfer from the throttles to the control column (which is a stick and not spectacles like the Beau) on take-off, so that the right hand may select wheels up, and then change back again. Switches are arranged in an unbroken row of eight or nine, so that it is not easy to find the correct one in the dark. The navigator and pilot sit side by side which, while being a welcome change for the navigator accustomed to the banishment of the rear fuselage of the Beaufighter, is too close for real comfort and causes our respective harnesses and Mae Wests to get hooked up from time to time. But the aircraft makes up for everything in its speed, climb, endurance and general handling.

8 September 1943
The Navy has a nightfighter development flight at Ford also, run by Major 'Skeets' Harris, a flying marine. We fly each other's aircraft a lot and help out on various trials. Today I fly their Fulmar and our Hurricane for the first time; neither is particularly impressive and I only wish we had a Spitfire.

Skeets's wife was a despatch rider with the WRNS and came from a well-to-do family; at this time she was not commissioned. On her occasional visits to Ford she was thus not supposed to join us socially in the officers' mess. Fortunately, her regulation navy-blue double-breasted jacket, breeches and black riding boots formed a sufficiently unusual uniform (it was really more like that of the SS than a Wren's, I suppose) for us to smuggle her into the bar, where her petite figure was immediately surrounded by FIU officers ready to close ranks at any attempt by sticklers for the book to be discourteous to the senior service.

Repercussions from the night I 'stole' my own Beaufighter filtered through to FIU after I had been there a week or so. Apparently nobody saw the funny side of it, let alone the serious gap in the airfield defence, but I am still sure that it was a good thing to have done (if a trifle foolhardy), particularly if things were tightened up as a result.

On 13 September I was promoted to the rank of flight lieutenant. Being a new boy I flew with any navigator, RAF or

RN, who was spare but gradually it became apparent that one recently arrived flying officer had no pilot of his own and we flew together quite frequently. We did a couple of defensive patrols and some general flying while I found my feet. We also started on a number of experimental flights: my introduction to AI Mk X (not yet in squadron service and with us for final evaluation), some high-level, bomber-support practices and a short attachment to AFDU (Air Fighting Development Unit, the day-fighter equivalent of ourselves) at Wittering to do some night trials with a gyro gunsight on a Lancaster target. But it was obvious that the spark wasn't there and after two months the navigator was tried by one or two of the more senior pilots before he eventually left us. At that time one of our senior pilots also left us and his navigator was without a driver. We crewed up together and there started a friendship which has lasted until the present. Flying Officer F. J. MacRae was thirty years old and doing a ground job as a flight lieutenant in 1941 when, driven by the same urges as I found myself, he asked to be transferred to flying duties. He had to go down two ranks to pilot officer before being trained as a radio operator and was then posted direct to FIU. Now thirty-two, he was over the average age for aircrew, a tall angular Scot with all the Scot's taciturn patriotism and quiet sense of humour. Mac and I got on very well from the start, and I was to find in my Scotsman a steady, reliable navigator, completely unflappable, with high technical ability and quiet persistence. He and his charming wife Violette were to remain happily married and, more than thirty years later, I am glad to have been godfather to their daughter as I was for Tony and Rosemary Nordberg.

The German nightfighter experimental unit, NJG.10 at Werneuchen, was meanwhile doing trials of its own. In their case it was a device designed to home on the 10cm transmissions of Bomber Command's *H2S* sets. Called *Naxos Z*, it achieved a range of ten miles on a captured *H2S* on its first flight on 11 September. On the ground, the German boffins had joined a *Würzburg* and a *Naxos* to give bearings on *H2S* transmissions at

150 miles; they were also experimenting with IFF tracking so that Bomber Command's raids were plotted as soon as they took off and switched on these two items of equipment. Early the following month a new form of German AI, called *SN2*, became operational. It gave improved maximum range and definition, but its minimum range was only 1,200ft. Efforts to reduce this failed to bear fruit for a long time, so that both the *SN2* for initial interception (it proved to be unjammed by *Window*) and *Lichtenstein* for final approach to visual were often carried by the same aircraft.

5 October 1943
Whiting *practice. This consists of allowing a fighter aircraft to come up behind on interception, until* Monica *tells us that he is 5,000– 6,000ft astern, and then whipping round in a tight turn. The idea is to get quickly out of the coverage of the German's AI (about 25° either side of the centre line) and then carry on turning until you wind up behind with him on your AI.* Monica *is a modified form of AI Mk IV and points straight backwards as a rear warner.*

We shall shortly be going over with the bombers, trying to look like a Lancaster on the German radar and hoping (!) to be intercepted by an enemy nightfighter. It seems to work. They will only allow AI Mk IV over Germany at the moment, but we hope that one of these days we may be allowed over with Mk VIII or even Mk X.

6 October 1943
AI Mk V [basically a Mk IV with an extra tube giving direct indication to the pilot] *practice. I don't see the point of looking into a CRT for a blip when the navigator is there to do that, and I can be looking out of the windscreen for the target visually.*

7 October 1943
I appear to have brought my jinx with me! Mac and I are on the defensive programme and there is a blitz on London. We get four contacts and are ordered off three of them for some reason; the fourth turns out to be a Wimpy.

10 October 1943

I fly the unit's Hornet Moth for the first time. This is a light, two-seater cabin biplane with side-by-side seating, about the size of a Tiger Moth. It is a most unorthodox aeroplane to have in a front-line unit, but we are an unorthodox unit. I see a Tiger Moth floating past and decide to have a bit of fun with what is presumably a pupil, so dive on him and pull gently round on his tail so as not to alarm him too much. In ten seconds he is on my tail and nothing I can do will shake him off; I eventually break it off and fly home much chastened. To my surprise he comes with me and even lands at Ford. I have been dogfighting with the station commander, who learned his air fighting on SE 5s the hard way and, failing a serviceable SE 5, is more at home in the Tiger Moth than anything else which flies.

18 October 1943

Bomber support to Hanover. Uneventful.

I wrote 'uneventful' against that log book entry, but I was at this time going through a difficult period. The cumulative effect of night flying in all weathers and of never having been over enemy territory before, worked on my nerves until I had a warning of the 'twitch'. But I had asked to join FIU to get some real operational flying and had only been there six weeks, so I couldn't cry off. It was a question of screwing myself up to concentrate on my flying and get on with the job. The weather was not good and I remember looking at the banks of dark clouds piled up in the eastern sky as twilight fell, and thinking that I would shortly have to fly through it all.

We had a bumpy climb to 20,000ft, largely on instruments, but found that we were clear of the main layer of cloud at that height. We set course for our target and skirted the few anvil-headed clouds which came up to our level. We got a good start from *Gee* (a grid-system navigation aid, it will be remembered) but soon we were flying on DR (dead reckoning) only, until ahead of us we could see redness glowing dully through the overcast. As we approached, the red area separated into

Page 85 (above) A rare photograph of the installation of AI Mk X presentation in a Mosquito; the rectangular faces of the two cathode-ray tubes may be compared with the drawing on page 66. The pilot's control column to the left gives an indication of the proximity of the two crewmen in the cramped cockpit; *(below)* self and Mac flying the captured Messerschmitt 410 painted in RAF prototype colours. The dive brakes are extended and the tail wheel has not fully retracted, which I have noted from other photographs is a fault also suffered by the Luftwaffe. The escort Mosquito Mk XVII houses AI Mk X under the bulbous nose; the crew flying it were to shoot down eight enemy aircraft and then go missing in the next two weeks

Page 86 (above) Junkers 88 nightfighter equipped with *Lichtenstein* AI;
(below) the *Lichtenstein* AI aerials on the nose of a Junkers 88

individual fires which, on yet closer investigation, flared up through gaps in the clouds. We could see the shock of individual bombloads exploding on the ground as the city of Hanover was systematically taken apart in an awesome demonstration of the destructive power of a modern air force. Bursts of flak speckled the sky over the target area and occasionally a flaming torch was lit as a bomber fell earthwards, cut down by flak or nightfighters.

We flew all round the edge of the target, with Mac searching the *Monica* rear warner and the AI for signs of the enemy, until the last aircraft had headed for home; all we saw was our own bombers. Fires continued to rage below us and could still be seen long after we had turned for base. I thrust into the back of my mind all thought of the misery and suffering going on below us as we concentrated on the return journey, checking off landmarks and enemy light beacons noted on the way out. I sweated like a bull for the entire trip and arrived back wringing wet. Uneventful indeed.

To this day I can recapture some of that atmosphere if the skies are stormy in the east at dusk, and if I let my mind wander back to those days of my first offensive operations.

21 October 1943
The AI Mk V fitted to a Mosquito now has windscreen projection of the pilot's tube. Without having to look down at the CRT, you can see the blip reflected in the windscreen with its little 'wings' growing as the range lessens. This makes a lot of difference, as the pilot doesn't have to stick his head inside the cockpit all the time. It only really works at night, however, as the projected image isn't bright enough to see in daylight.

Had a few jugs in the mess with the Navy in memory of Nelson. They have a good song to the tune of 'Billikins and his Dinah', which goes:

> *They say in the Raff that a landing's OK*
> *If the pilot can get up and still walk away,*
> *But in the Fleet Air Arm the prospect is grim,*
> *You look such a clot if the pilot can't swim.*
>
> *Cracking show! I'm alive!*

But I've still got to render my A.25 [accident report form].

If you come o'er the round-down and you see Wings's frown
You can safely assume that your hook isn't down;
A bloody great barrier looms up on high
And you hear Wings shout: 'Switch off your engine or die!'
   Cracking show! I'm alive!
   But I've still got to render my A.25.

I thought I was coming in low enough but . . .
I was fifty feet up when the batsman said: 'Cut!'
Loud in my ear'oles the sweet angels sang:
'Float, float, you bastard you'll certainly PRANG!'
   Cracking show! I'm alive!
   But I've still got to render my A.25.

NFIU introduced us to a variation of their field gun race, which is put on at displays and tattoos. In the real thing a gun is dismantled by each of two teams, ferried across an imaginary river and reassembled on the other side in a race. We played it in the ante-room with service iron bedsteads. Two teams of three start on opposite sides of the room, dismantle the bed and then have to carry one of their number on the spring part while they hold the separate head and foot pieces. They proceed down opposite sides of the room over suitably placed obstacles such as chairs, tables, etc. The interest centres on the point at the far end of the room at which they must cross over to continue back the other side, before reassembling their bed. A major obstacle such as a couple of sofas is positioned at this point to cause as tight a bottleneck as possible as the two teams struggle to get past each other. As you lose points for every time you drop your passenger, there is a certain amount of pushing and shoving as the two teams meet. It was great fun and we suffered remarkably few casualties.

22 October 1943
Patrol Blackgang GCI. Mac and I coax the old Beau up to 24,000ft,
which is no mean achievement. It is bloody cold and doesn't do us any
good except keep us out of the top of the cu-nimb with all its turbulence

Togs' father was a regular air force officer who had been on Sopwith Camels in 209 Squadron in World War I, and had flown with Captain Brown on the sortie of 21 April 1918, when the German air ace von Richtofen had been shot down. Togs was red-headed, with all the fire and enthusiasm which that usually means.

10 November 1943
To Defford with George Cooke, CO of the Nav/Rad school where Tony is, and with Frank Clarke, our Special Signals Officer. We drive from Defford to TRE at Malvern and have a fascinating day talking about AI Mk IX which has been revived [development had been stopped when the American SCR 720, or AI Mk X, proved so successful]. *We meet a lot of boffins and I find that I can understand them when they remember that I am only a pilot and not a walking sliderule. They seem interested to hear our views as users, for this shows them the ultimate requirements.*

15 November 1943
For some extraordinary reason Fighter Command has been renamed Air Defence of Great Britain. What a mouthful and what a crime to chuck away all that tradition.

The renaming of Fighter Command had something to do with the reorganisation of the chain of command in connection with the invasion of Europe, now planned for the following year.

We flew several more *Mahmoud* high-level bomber support sorties that winter, trying to be intercepted as a bomber and then doing a *Whiting* onto the enemy fighter's tail so that our AI Mk IV could pick up a contact which could be brought to a visual. The weather was never particularly good for our trips and I found that I was always too pre-occupied with keeping the Mosquito on an even keel to say that I enjoyed them. Mac was as imperturbable as ever and to this day I don't know whether he was aware of the silent struggle which was going on within me. He got us there and back and I put the aircraft down in one bit, but that's about all I can say—except that Mac forgot his parachute on one of our trips, to Frankfurt I think it was. He never told me at the time and said afterwards that he had resigned himself to jumping out without it if it came to the push.

I can't pretend that these trips were particularly well organised and I seldom knew what was really likely to happen, exactly where the bomber stream was, how high or how fast. We were all hoping that the intelligence boys had done their homework properly and had given us a good track to follow. I had a vague idea that the enemy used some sort of beacon to assemble his nightfighters, but what they were like or where they were I had little idea. Added to that, we were a bit fast to look like a Lancaster on the German plot, and we were not emitting $H2S$ signals, so the Germans were never really fooled; perhaps this explains why we saw nothing of the Luftwaffe—though we had plenty of visuals on our own bombers, looking so vulnerable as they flew steadily and unsuspectingly with us 200ft behind and below, in the darkness.

The Mosquito was a comfortable aircraft after the Beaufighter. As I have said, the cockpit layout was not so good and it was a little cramped to have to sit so close to one's navigator, but the machine was smooth and stable, and could be trimmed to fly almost 'hands off' in good weather. Above all, somebody had at last realised that warmth was not necessarily bad for discipline; a crew able to fly without additional thick jackets, sweaters and gloves was not decadent but a good deal more efficient. Also the fact that the crew could see and touch each other helped companionship and morale.

One way that the Mosquito was worse than the Beaufighter was in providing defence against a groundcrew torch. On going out to your aircraft at night, your eyes slowly adapted to night vision so that, by the time you settled into your seat, you had achieved about 80 per cent adaptation to the dark. It was then the job of the groundcrew to shut the door and see that it was securely fastened. As like as not one of them would come busily

6 RADAR GADGETRY

1 January 1944
Mac is a holy terror at Hogmanay. He managed to get hold of a couple of bottles of whisky last night, thrust one into my hand and said, 'Come on, Jerry, let's see the New Year in properly.' My head this morning tells me that we did.

4 January 1944
After a fruitless defensive patrol of 3½ hours in a Mosquito off the south coast, Mac and I are scrambled for a second patrol after we landed and were looking forward to bed. We cause a certain amount of alarm and despondency to a Lancaster from the Bomber Development Unit, here for trials on the extended corkscrew evasion. He is busy taxiing out to the eastern end of our east/west runway, which has been given him for take-off, when the unit's Typhoon takes off south/north on a scramble with AI Mk VI (the wind is more truly from the north and he is happier into wind on the short runway). As he goes off the Lanc is at the northern end of this runway and is told to wait while the Typhoon flashes past his nose. He then waddles on to the far end of the east/west runway, only to see yet another aircraft roar past his nose taking-off towards him as Mac and I scramble downwind from the nearest point to our dispersal because there is not enough wind to worry us. A rather shaken Lanc asks if he is really at the correct take-off point and is told that he is, indeed, the only one in step. His opinion of Fighter Command as a rather light-hearted bunch is presumably reinforced by this seemingly irresponsible attitude to aerodrome procedure.

We are vectored after a bogey and I suddenly see a light passing through the sky at about five miles range. The rumours have been circulating again of an elaborate German trap, whereby British nightfighters chase after these lights never to be heard of again; there is another German aircraft flying along behind ready to shoot down the RAF fighter. The CO of 29 Squadron based at Ford went missing recently in just this manner. So we point our nose at the airspace behind the light and search for the snake in the grass. There is no joy, and at that moment, the light goes out. I hastily point the aircraft towards his last seen position but Mac gets no contact, despite a thorough search all round. We have wasted a good opportunity.

We are then warned from the ground that another aircraft is coming up astern of us. As we have no rear warner, this is disconcerting to say the least, and the events of the evening have combined to produce a state of jitters, in my half of the cockpit at any rate.

'He's about half a mile astern of you now and overtaking,' says Skyblue control.

My mouth goes dry and my heels drum on the floor by the rudder pedals. Then I get a hold of myself and decide that we must turn towards the side on which the enemy is approaching rather than away from him, if we are to snap round onto his tail quickly.

'What shall I do?' I request feebly, wanting to learn which way to turn.

'Take the appropriate action,' replies Skyblue sensibly.

I decide that there may not be much time left to sort out the misunderstanding, so wind the Mossie round in a tight turn to port. We fail to pick up a contact and, after three or four circuits, Skyblue assures us that there is nothing there any more. Whether there ever was anything, or whether it has decided to go home as soon as it realised that we are not sitting ducks, and got swallowed up in the general chaos, we never find out.

In addition to such night flying as was required by the trials programme, FIU was still putting two aircraft on the defensive state each night, taking turns for the sort of patrol described above. This used up a certain amount of manpower but at least it kept us in touch with the requirement. It also made us respected by the squadrons, so that they were more ready to accept our recommendations. We reported to dispersal in the services of Jimmy Rawnsley, on rest from his second tour of operations. John Cunningham had gone as Group Captain Night Ops to HQ 11 Group at Uxbridge and Jimmy brought his infectious enthusiasm and wise counsel to us. At the same time the unit was moved to Wittering to make way at Ford for the short-range, day-fighter squadrons which would be covering the invasion of Europe. We started training for low-level intruder operations, which would involve flying to German nightfighter airfields to catch them landing back after RAF Bomber Command had turned for home. Low-looking AI Mk X was to be permitted to fly over enemy territory for these operations. We went on several low-level night cross-countries, finishing at friendly aerodromes who had been warned of our intentions, so that we could intercept aircraft on their circuit.

One of the requirements before the invasion took place was to knock out the German radar chain. There was still the *Himmelbett* system deployed round the Dutch, Belgian and French coasts, which could not only detect aircraft but also shipping, and you may remember that its main radars were the *Freya* and the *Würzburg*. The former was large and easily found from the air but the *Würzburg* was small and took some locating, so it was decided to install a homing device in a Typhoon. In this way one aircraft could home on the enemy transmitting station, guiding a formation of ground-attack Typhoons right to their target with smoke bombs.

The job was given to us and we didn't much like the idea on two counts, neither of which could be expected to weigh very heavily with 'their Airships'. First, there was all that water to cross on one engine (the day boys used to do it every day but, when you have been brought up on twins, there is something rather naked about a single engine over the sea: we always used to consider that you could tell as soon as you crossed the coast in a single-engined aircraft—the engine used to start to sound rough). Secondly, there would be no nice protecting screen of darkness to hide us from all those angry Germans in their FW 190s and ME 109s.

99

Chris Hartley went up to Scotland with a Typhoon which had *Abdullah* homer equipment fitted, as it was code-named. He did trials with a *Würzburg* which had been captured in North Africa and, to everyone's delight except ours, he pronounced the idea feasible; indeed, accuracy was within 100yd.

A special flight of some half a dozen Typhoons was established at Holmsley South in the New Forest in southern England, and Teddy Daniel went down with three other pilots to run it.

The great day came for the first operational sortie and the Germans proved themselves more astute than the British scientists who had thought up the scheme gave them credit for. They employed the perfect countermeasure: on the indication of a low-flying fast formation making straight for them, they adopted the very sensible ruse of switching off their radar when the plot got within ten miles. The affair fizzled out, much to our undisguised delight, and other ways were found of dealing with these targets before D-Day.

In April another new unit was added to RAF strength: the Bomber Support Development Unit started life at Foulsham. This was an offspring of 100 Group and we recognised the hand of Rory Chisholm in it. At all events, it took some of the fast-increasing load off our shoulders. For instance, we no longer had anything to do with *Serrate* in any of its forms. This was the device for homing onto *Lichtenstein* and *SN2* AI transmissions which, because of the desire to keep the Germans guessing as to how much we knew about their wavelengths, was developed as far away from their monitoring stations as possible; it had started flying trials at Drem in Scotland under the guidance of Derek Jackson (who also had a lot to do with the evolution of *Window*, which he had been pushing out of the target Beaufighter which, relatively speaking, had got away with it when the first AI Mk IX had been shot down by a Spitfire at Christmas 1942).

No account of radar and countermeasures would be complete without a mention of this remarkable figure, who had earned a DFC flying as a radio operator with 604 in the early days, before returning later to his test tubes. I can but quote from Jimmy Rawnsley's book, *Night Fighter*, to give a succinct description of the man.

> Derek Jackson . . . was a University professor, a physicist of world-wide repute and a hard riding amateur jockey who had risked his neck in the Grand National . . . He was one of the prize finds in the great drive to recruit master brains for our new trade.
> Jackson had the mind of the first-rate scientist, detached and objective in his approach to his job, and his interceptions became polished and balanced exercises. To him, an enemy aircraft bristling with lethal weapons was merely an object in the sky whose relative position and movement were to be determined by an exact and precise use of the cathode ray tubes with which he was so familiar. It may have all been a trade to us: to Jackson it was a science and, because of the complex nature of the man, perhaps in some ways an art.

In this art, Jackson relegated the pilot to the function of being merely another control knob at his finger tips.

'Pilot, turn left,' he would say in his clipped, imperious manner. 'Harder. Throttle back, pilot. Steady as you go, pilot.'

It may have been effective, an art, a science, and brilliant, but it was maddening to be turned into a glorified taxi driver, however appropriate.

BSDU took over many of the devices which were designed to make life more difficult for the German night defences.

ASH entered squadron service with the RAF two months later under the guise of AI Mk XV and was used by three squadrons on bomber support. This was a 3cm AI of which great things were expected but which never really lived up to its promise. At any rate, BSDU now dealt with it, apart from any flying we may have done for NFIU (it was also destined for the navy). *Perfectos* was also largely taken off our programme. This has been described, in *Instruments of Darkness* by Alfred Price, as one of the neatest electronic gadgets to come out of World War II; it sent out radar pulses designed to trigger the IFF sets of all German aircraft in the area. The returning signals gave direction, distance and, since they had to be emanating from German aircraft, positive identification as hostile. Its introduction led to a wide-scale abandonment of IFF by the Germans, which all helped to create problems for their control organisation.

8 April 1944
Bomber Development Unit Lancaster affiliation. Extended corkscrew. There is no doubt that this form of evasion is first class, for it ensures that the nightfighter almost always ends by hanging on its props underneath the Lanc and to one side—just where the mid-upper gunner likes 'em. It takes a lot out of a pilot and makes it difficult to maintain a decent course but, if only the bomber boys could be made to understand what sitting ducks they are on a dark night, perhaps more of them would use the standard corkscrew. This is good evasion as we have shown with Peter Cribb's boys (BDU), and should be routine drill over enemy territory even if the extended version can't be.

It was revealed in interrogation of Luftwaffe nightfighter pilots after the war that many of them broke off an interception if they considered that the target was evading, and went to look for easier meat—of which there was, unfortunately, plenty.

5 May 1944
To Defford via Long Marston—unintentionally. A sharp rainstorm causes me to lose my way for the first time ever on a daylight cross-country. Have the ignominious experience of circling the airfield several times while trying to sort myself out, then landing and going to flying control to ask where I am. Shall never hear the last of this from Mac when I return. Pick up Teddy and David Crerar and on to Yeovil, where Teddy and I are to collect a couple of Westland Welkin high altitude fighters. They have twin Merlin 77s with special superchargers, pressurised cockpits and are designed to beat the Junkers 86P, which comes over every so often on a PR job at around 35,000ft. We are to fly them by night for evaluation.

Page 103 (above) A Heinkel 111 modified to carry the flying bomb (FZG 76) for air launching. Some aircraft carried them under the port wing, but the two I saw operationally appeared to have them as shown above. Note the tubing for the starting mechanism coming from the side of the aircraft; *(right)* AI being serviced on a Messerschmitt 110 G4. The small aerials are those of *Lichtenstein* and the large ones are *SN2*

Page 104 Self and Mac at the wedding of his daughter (and my god-daughter) in 1972

Westlands give us lunch at a hotel in Yeovil, where local residents look askance at the brutal and licentious soldiery invading their sanctum. I must say, we weren't expecting such a slap-up welcome and we have got our flying battledress on. The waiter is dressed in tails and nearly dies when I ask him if the salmon is fresh; apparently they never serve anything from tins. Don't know how they do it.

After seeing round the factory, we are shown the tits on the Welkin by Harald Penrose, the Chief Test Pilot, and I am off first. I circle waiting for Teddy who takes-off, does half a circuit and lands again immediately. I shrug my shoulders and set off for Wittering without him. When he eventually turns up he tells how his fuel gauges were reading zero when he got into the cockpit.

'That's OK,' says Penrose. 'Somebody connected them up the wrong way round yesterday, so you'll find they say zero when tanks are full and vice versa. Your chaps can soon sort it out when you get the aircraft to Wittering.'

What he doesn't know is that somebody has already sorted it out, and the tanks really are empty. Teddy gets to about 100ft and one engine coughs and cuts out, so he turns smartly downwind to get back in again. The engine picks up but then the other one goes, and they do this on and off until he gets down, all in one piece. Red faces from Westlands and, when she has been filled, Harald Penrose takes her up and gives Teddy his own private air display just to show that there is nothing else wrong with her.

8 May 1944
Altitude climb in the Welkin. I get to 40,000ft in nineteen minutes, which is a minute less than I took to get to 30,000ft in a Mossie Mk IX with Bill Maguire the other day—and we thought we were doing well then! They'd get a better performance from the Welkin if they didn't load it down with a lot of unnecessary weight. They were so proud of the ¼in armour plate behind the pilot's seat when we saw over the factory. But who's going to shoot at you from behind when you're at angels forty? Certainly not a JU 86P; we hope we'll be behind him. It is a clear day and, from 43,000ft over the middle of England, I can see the North Sea on one side and the Irish Sea on the other at the same time.

The elevator trim is electrically operated so that the control can pass through the wall of the pressurised cockpit, and it fails to trim tail heavy. I don't discover this until I have wound on quite a bit of nose-heavy trim experimentally; my arm is aching by the time I have lost all that height hauling back on the stick all the way down.

The few sorties carried out by the JU 86P resulted in quite an effort from the British aircraft industry to combat the threat. Apart from the Welkin, a special variant of the Mosquito, the Mk XV, was developed (the prototype was a mixture of various aircraft and flew in just over a week from the initial order). This had two Merlin 77s with four-bladed airscrews, a pressurised cabin, an extra 5ft of wingspan and, most sensibly, a considerable reduction in weight. Production aircraft had AI Mk VIII for the night threat, but were reduced to two machine-guns instead of four cannons, on the assumption that these would be enough to force the enemy down to lower levels by puncturing his pressurisation, if nothing else. The Mosquito XV flew to 43,000ft, which was not far short of the Welkin's ceiling, and got there nearly as quickly.

Jimmy Rawnsley was suddenly posted to 11 Group headquarters about now, with promotion to squadron leader. We were sorry to see him go, but John Cunningham wanted him and could get him the well-deserved promotion, so off he went.

24 May 1944
I am asked to take a WAAF signals officer for a flight in a Mosquito to show her how the SCR 729 [a special radar set for receiving beacons and IFF interrogation, used in conjunction with AI Mks VIII and X, which did not have this facility otherwise] *she looks after functions in the air. She is quite a popsy and I can't resist the temptation to show off a little. I boast about the Mosquito's single-engine performance and then feather the starboard engine, or at least I press the button. The propeller goes into a semi-feathered condition and then won't go further or come out again. The aircraft won't maintain height like this and it is 1 May 1942 all over again, only this time we are over land*

and, more to the point, just high enough to get back to Wittering. I don't want to alarm my fair passenger, so pretend that there is nothing wrong and head back for base. Flight Officer Wrigley must be unduly stupid if she doesn't realise something's up, the way I break off my chatty conversation with her, call for a homing and keep fiddling hopefully with the engine controls. We reach the airfield with enough height to get in on a straight approach slightly across the grass runway. We are 400ft up, wheels and flaps down, when I see a Hurricane of AFDU just above us to our left on final approach to the correct runway. We are converging so that we shall probably meet at or just after the point of touchdown.

'Hurricane on the approach,' I call on the local frequency, keeping my voice slow and elaborately calm. 'Are you receiving? Lighthouse 37 over.'

'Hello, Lighthouse 37,' he replies. 'Poker 29 receiving you loud and clear. Over.'

'I'm sorry to bother you,' I say, determined not to show any signs of worry in front of my WAAF. 'But I wonder whether you'd mind going round again. I'm crossing you from starboard and can't go round myself as I'm on one engine. Over.'

'OK, 37. But I'm on one engine too,' he replies with a chuckle as his wheels come up and he flies across in front of us.

'Thank you so much,' I answer with studied calm. 'Much obliged.' And I was, for we'd have been in for an interesting time if he'd been on another frequency and not able to hear me. When we have parked and got out of the aircraft, I apologise to the WAAF and say that there was a little trouble with the starboard engine.

'Yes, I know,' she says prettily and off she goes.

6 June 1944
The invasion has been on since dawn. Centimetric AI has been released for operations over enemy territory and Mac and I fly an intruder to Orléans/Bricy with AI Mk VIII. I don't know whether it is the lay-off from offensive ops for a while, the better weather of the summer months, or the fact that this trip is a low-level one so that we don't have to climb up through all that cu-nimb, but I find that I no longer have that feeling of awful finality as the aircraft door is shut before take-off; I realise after a short while in the air that I am not sweating. There is considerable com-

fort to be had from knowing exactly where you are all the time. We navigate on a system of straight legs between major landmarks, usually water, and find that we can map read quite easily if the moon is three-quarters full or more and there is not full cloud cover.

Orléans/Bricy is darkened when we reach it at midnight and there is no activity during our hour on duty. We set course for the first landmark on the way home and then see a German signal cartridge fired off to quieten a searchlight well over to port. We turn port and get a contact at two miles and well above, which Mac quickly brings to a visual at 3,000ft range. We close in underneath, discussing the identity of the other aircraft; Mac refusing to believe it is a Hun. I am happy in my own mind that it is a Heinkel 177, but want confirmation from Mac, so I go in to 100yd, right underneath. From that position we can even see the black crosses on the wings and Mac is convinced. Thank God it is not a Heinkel 111, which we have all been forbidden to attack. From below in the dark, a Dakota can look very like an HE 111 and there are so many Daks around while the invasion is on that nobody is taking any chances—the odds are about 100 to 1 that any HE 111 is, in fact, a Dakota.

We drop back to 200yd and I fire a 2sec burst at his port engine. There is an immediate flash and a large piece falls away. The HE 177 then swings hard port and dives steeply. I throttle back but overshoot nevertheless, giving a 1sec burst as we go by.

As he drops below our nose there is a bright glare, which I think at first means that he is on fire but which turns out to be a signal flare. The Luftwaffe has, as we do, about half-a-dozen different combinations of coloured lights, and a particular combination is allotted to each particular period of the twenty-four hours as a recognition signal; the combination changes every four hours. We always carry the German-type cartridges with us for use in emergency; they are numbered from 1 to 6 and called ESN cartridges (enemy signal numbers). Somewhere in the Luftwaffe organisation—I imagine he must be a French office worker on some airfield in occupied France—there is a brave Allied agent who makes it his regular business to discover the code for the following twenty-four hours and transmit it to England, so that we frequently know which ESN to use at which period. We do not compromise this information by flying around enemy territory displaying our knowledge by always having the correct cartridge up the spout, but we are ready to select the right one if necessary. If an enemy aircraft has fired the colours of the period near to us, then obviously we can show just cause for knowing the colours.

I lose sight of the big Heinkel in the haze but Mac maintains contact at 2,000ft range and well below. We drop down quickly and he disappears in the ground returns, which are temporarily intensified as we point the nose down; when we level out he has gone and we never get him again. Some searchlights start probing the darkness two or three miles away, but they douse when another ESN is fired; we try to get a contact on whoever they are investigating but the only result is that they come on again, looking for us this time. Mac shoots off an ESN and, lo and behold, the lights go out.

We then get a contact and close on an aircraft flying south-west at about 3,000ft and weaving gently. This turns out to be a Liberator so we pull away before he sees us and lets us have it; presumably a supply dropper for the Maquis. We go and have another look at the aerodrome we have just left, partly to see if they are landing our HE 177 and partly to give us a firm landmark to start from on our journey. We cross out of the French coast at Point d'Ailly, well to the east of the invasion beachhead and cannot see any fireworks. But they must be sweating it out down there and many on both sides will be dying. Not for the first time I reflect upon my good fortune at not having to slog it out with the army, creeping forward through mud and rubble expecting death at every hedgerow and street corner. I know that shameful fear would turn my belly to water and rob me of self control, as the deadly game of hide and seek was grimly acted out. We at least are slightly more masters of our own fate and are remote from the immediate din and shock of battle. We do our fighting sitting down and come back to a bath and clean sheets. I am certain that this is the only way I could play an honourable part in this nightmare, and am glad to have forced my unwilling body to do its duty; unlike Shakespeare's 'gentlemen in England now a'bed', if I survive I shall not have to think myself accurs'd I was not here, nor hold my manhood cheap while any speaks that fought with us upon invasion day.

We land back at Manston and put in our combat report. Micky Phillips is back already and tells us that we have been on transmit ever since we took off! Some fault in the R/T box has meant that we have been broadcasting everything we said in the cockpit from the moment we became airborne. (This explains why we couldn't get any reply from flying control when we asked permission to land.) While Mac and I were debating the identity of our HE 177, Micky was apparently certain that he was the aircraft we were looking at, so he flew straight and level to give us a good chance to identify him. When I said to Mac that I could see the black crosses on it, Micky thought I was looking at his drop tanks and got really worried. On hearing that we were about to open fire he reared up, peeled off to port and dived for the ground with everything twitching! We were jolly lucky that the Hun didn't use our transmissions to get a fix on us and send someone to intercept us.

An AI nightfighter's main task over enemy territory was to use its airborne radar to seek out and then intercept enemy aircraft so that they could be destroyed. Besides the engines and vast quantities of fuel to give it range and endurance (fighter versions of the Mosquito could carry over 750gal of fuel), the Mosquito's main equipment comprised airborne radar in several forms. This complex electronic weapon filled most of the front end of the aeroplane and a large part of the fuselage (except for four 20mm cannons which lay with their ammunition in the belly); its controls and indicator units took up a great deal of the room in the already cramped cockpit. Besides the AI itself, our machines had *Gee* for navigation, SCR 729 for picking up homing beacons and blind-approach beacons, *Monica* for tail warning, *Perfectos* for homing onto the Luftwaffe IFF sets, our own IFF set, and two four-channel R/T sets. Some aircraft of 100 Group also carried *Serrate* for homing onto the German nightfighter's radar transmissions, and infra-red identification equipment.

Mac's main job was operation and interpretation of all this equipment, with the solitary exception of the R/T. Navigation was only an incidental and, as I had more time to spare for looking outside the cockpit, I did most of the map reading. To facilitate this we would devote a lot of attention to pre-flight planning, by marking the appropriate 1:500,000 scale maps

with pencilled tracklines joining the major landmarks we pro-
posed using (avoiding as much as possible the nasty hatched
red areas which represented known flak zones); these tracks had
cross lines marked on them at five-minute intervals as a check
on the time. I would then orientate the map so that our track
was pointing the way we were going and check our progress
along it, occasionally dragging Mac away from his black boxes
to confirm or refute a particular wood or town and to remind
me of our ETA (expected time of arrival) at the next turning
point.

He kept a log on his knee pad, which had paper on a roller,
and he had a Dalton navigation computer for working out new
courses if the forecast wind proved wildly wrong and required an
alteration of course greater than the 5–10° estimate at which
we became highly accurate. If we were taken away from our
planned route—perhaps by an AI chase—and he needed to
draw new tracklines on the map, Mac had to spread it on his
knees underneath the AI indicator unit with its gain, tuning,
frequency, and range controls, vertical-sweep selector switches
and indicator-tube visors (no chart table for him, there wasn't
room). The track had to be hurriedly drawn and measured, the
angle and airspeed added to the wind speed (either forecast or
freshly calculated by Mac), and the new course and ground
speed worked out together with a new ETA. All this had to be
done between keeping an eye on the AI, our tail warner and
anything else I might cook up for him. It was then my job to fly
the course accurately (to within 2° at most, preferably 1°), and
at the correct airspeed and also to keep an eye on fuel consump-
tion and the clock.

10 June 1944
Peter Twiss [later chief test pilot for Fairey Aviation and some-
time holder of the world's air speed record in the Fairey Delta;
he shot down three German aircraft while flying our Mosquitos],
*one of the navy pilots, got a JU 88 last night on intruder with Denis
Lake in one of our Mosquitos. The Navy certainly gets the better deal*

over our mutual swapping of aircraft; nobody could pretend that a Firefly is as much fun to fly as a Mosquito and it would never be able to catch a JU 88 even if it found one. As for the Fulmar . . .!

11 June 1944
Flower [code-name for low-level intruder on enemy airfields] *to Laon and Juvincourt with AI Mk VIII. Weather very bad, but manage to find both airfields. VL* [visual Lorenz bad-weather landing lights] *is lit at former and the perimeter-track lights at latter. No activity.*

13 June 1944
The first Diver, or pilotless aircraft, nicknamed doodlebug by the Press, falls between Dartford and Gravesend.

22 June 1944
We have a white Wimpy from Coastal Command, with equipment called H2D. It is meant to detect movement on land, on a similar principle to H2S. I fly it for the first time and, as it is a sunny day and there are plenty of people with nothing better to do, I take ten passengers with me, including an operator for the H2D and also including the WRNS Adjutant of NFIU: Third Officer Elizabeth Chandler no less. The H2D seems to detect cows and telegraph poles as readily as it detects transport on the roads, and it all looks alike to it. We decide that the toss of a coin would give more reliable results, but the authorities are not convinced and make us keep the beast for a little longer.

Elizabeth Chandler was the only member of the women's services we didn't include when we used to sing 'Good night ladies' in the bar towards the end of a noisy evening. Not because she wasn't a lady, but because she was so much part of our lives that we paid her the compliment of treating her as one of us. She didn't always stay, but she drank beer with us, swore (mildly) with us, sang with us and pub crawled with us. She always gave the impression of gaiety and good humour, and she brought just a little softness into the sometimes brittle and superficial existence we led. She was a tower of strength to NFIU (although I rather suspect that she wept privately for those of us who failed to return from operations), getting them all of, and more than, their entitlement to the perks we all clamoured for. She had a difficult job organising a naval unit on an RAF station, but she did it well.

'We don't do that in the Royal Navy,' was one of her stock ways of getting round particularly irksome RAF regulations. She was equally ready to turn a Nelsonian eye to naval rules and, if you were desperate for transport for a particular job, you could usually count on borrowing the NFIU Utilicon van. I don't think she had any enemies, and she 'mothered' us all impartially, if such a word can be used of someone who was our own age.

24 June 1944
Peter Twiss does an upward Charlie in the Welkin low down over our dispersal as I am taxiing out for an NFT. I have to show that the RAF can do what the Navy can do, so, as soon as we are airborne, I do one myself in the Mossie; it is rather ropey, so I do another which is a bit better. Both Mac and I, however, hope that the Navy isn't starting a competition for the most dangerous manoeuvre.

Flower *to Chateauroux with AI Mk X. We fly to Manston to refuel as usual, as this will give us greater range, and find after take-off from there that we are flying through thick cloud with heavy electrical discharges flickering up and down the windscreen and making circles of fire round the tips of each propeller—St Elmo's fire, as we call it. On the other hand it is soon apparent that there aren't many volts on board the aircraft, and I suspect that we have been struck by lightning. Not to put too fine a point on it, our generator has obviously packed up. We are always allowed absolute discretion as to whether we press on or turn back when problems occur. The dividing line between sensible discretion and the dreaded 'lack of moral fibre' is a narrow one, however, and nobody wants to permit an accusing finger to be pointed in his direction. We have no lighting, no intercom, no* Gee, *no AI and no R/T. There is a major electrical storm still raging furiously round us and we are soon hopelessly lost, with no means of calling for radio assistance; in addition I doubt whether our cannons, which are fired electrically, will work. I don't check in case they do and spoil my feeling of justification in abandoning the trip somewhere over northern France. We get back to Manston, circle it in the dark and fire off the colours of the period on the approach; we get a green and land OK.*

We are taxiing round the perimeter track when we feel a shuddering at the back of the aircraft. This turns out to be a Royal Navy Grumman Avenger getting familiar at the expense of quite a chunk of our tail unit. Bloody fool was obviously going too fast and, to make it more stupid, we find that our navigation lights are, in fact, working so he has no excuse.

7 FLYING BOMBS

Flying bombs started arriving in the London area in quantity from 15 June onwards. HQ Air Defence of Great Britain ordered its pre-arranged defence plan into effect. Guns, balloons and fighters were deployed in belts along the southern approaches to London. These defences were to destroy over 4,000 flying bombs; only some 2,400 were to reach the Greater London area.

The fastest fighter in the RAF in any numbers at that time was the Hawker Tempest. It alone had any reasonable margin of speed over the jet-driven bombs which streamed over our coasts at speeds varying between 320 and 350mph and between 2,000 and 3,000ft. But invasion needs were paramount and only one wing of Tempests could be spared to combat the new menace. Spitfires and Mustangs by day and Mosquitos by night were thrown into the battle. Results were achieved by stripping all armour and unnecessary external fittings from the aircraft; high-grade fuel was used to get more power from protesting engines; and the pilots patrolled at a height from which they could dive on their targets to gain speed.

It was decided to supplement the Mosquitos at night with some Tempests. The wing at Newchurch, a small grass airfield on top of Beachy Head, already fiercely engaged by day, was asked to fly as many night patrols as their exhausted pilots could manage.

It was soon apparent that day-fighter pilots were not sufficiently at home in the dark clouds of night, because they did not have the necessary experience on instruments. Poor visibility and restricted navigational aids made night flying hazardous unless blind flying was almost second nature (the German *Wilde Sau* single-engined, night-flying fighters had experienced the same problems, losing more aircraft through flying accidents than from British bomber gunners). Absorbed in a violent chase, a pilot would not know where he was being led; the only aid to help him find his unfamiliar way back to Newchurch was a radio homer.

It was decided to see whether nightfighter pilots could more easily convert to the Tempest than day-fighter pilots could convert to all-weather night flying. We at FIU were ordered to convert some of our pilots to the Tempest. Because they had both flown on the abortive *Abdullah* experiment with Typhoons (an aircraft not unlike the Tempest), Teddy Daniel, the flight commander, and Flight Lieutenant Joe Berry, a pilot whom Chris Hartley had managed to grab on his return from the Mediterranean theatre of operations, were the first two. They became the nucleus of a small Tempest detachment which was to shoot down more than eighty flying bombs in seven weeks.

On 25 June the two pilots arrived at Newchurch in brand-new aircraft. Some dozen airmen were sent by road, to provide the ground party. They set up their tented camp a little apart from the resident day wing, who seemed to regard them with tolerant scorn.

The weather immediately showed signs of what it had in store. Low cloud and rain prevented flying on the first three nights.

Teddy and Joe suffered some leg-pulling in the bar of the officers' mess tent. The other pilots were somewhat relieved that the newcomers were also human. Nightfighter pilots, they jeered, could not fly any more than anyone else when the cloud was on the deck.

On 28 June the clouds lifted a little and the FIU pilots held a conference. The gibes they had suffered were not to be borne another night, so they would go and have a look at the weather. Teddy ordered the covers off the aircraft and they started getting ready to fly. Looking up they could see nothing but an unbroken expanse of low cloud scudding by.

The other pilots had not noticed the departure of the pair. In the bar at dusk, the noise of laughter and talk was suddenly shattered by the familiar blast of a Tempest engine. In the silence which followed, the second aircraft added its raucous crackle.

Unconscious of the ripple they had caused, Joe followed his flight commander to the end of the line of flares. He saw Teddy's aircraft straighten up, pause and then disappear down the flarepath into the murk. He taxied forward, opened the throttle and gathered speed down the runway.

Before the last flare had flashed past he was airborne. Wheels up; throttle back; adjust airscrew pitch. The vital drill came automatically as he concentrated on keeping his aircraft climbing on instruments. He changed from aerodrome frequency to sector control. Teddy Daniel's voice crackled through his headphones, acknowledging instructions; there was evidently plenty of trade. In turn he was vectored towards the south.

Soon he climbed through the top of the low-cloud layer, with further broken cloud piled up above him. He flew along in a gap between the layers and could now afford to look outside his cockpit. Suddenly he spotted a flickering yellow glow away to the south over the English Channel. Streaking along was his first flying bomb.

'Tally ho!' He took over control of the interception. All too quickly he found that seeing the target was one thing, destroying it another. Control had to be accurate, the engagement swift, otherwise he found himself flying through the lethal AA gun belt. Even when well placed to attack, his vision was blotted out by the blinding glare of the *Diver*'s exhaust so that it was hard to see the target's shape to gauge its range. He longed for the help of the Mosquito's AI; instead he turned up the power of his gunsight bulb and tried to sight through the graticule.

They both flew three times that night and they both destroyed two flying bombs. The weather remained fickle over the ensuing days and the two pilots were often kept out of the air, but they flew whenever it was at all possible. Joe's favourite technique was to fly some 4,000ft above the usual target height and, on sighting the now familiar yellow flame, he turned onto the same course and let the missile overtake him underneath. As it passed, he pushed the stick forward and came down on it with the superior speed conferred by his dive. He drew alongside so as to keep out of its slipstream and only at the last moment did he pull into the turbulent wake of the hot air from the tailpipe.

The bad weather continued into July. On the second night of the month, Joe got too close to one bomb as it blew up in front of him. Immediately he felt the thud of metal striking his aircraft. The motor faltered, picked up and spluttered along uncertainly. Now was the time when he would have liked a second engine, but that one got him back all right. The same thing happened to Teddy Daniel three nights later but he was not so lucky. In between selecting targets from the salvoes of missiles, Joe listened to the drama on his radio.

'My engine has failed. I am ten miles south of Beachy Head.' Teddy's familiar voice sounded unruffled. The controller asked his height and, when Joe heard that he was at 3,000ft he knew that he would never reach land.

'Bale out, Teddy,' he chipped in. 'Bale out.'

'I'm going to do just that. I'll leave my transmitter on for a fix. Cheerio.'

'Cheerio. We'll have you picked up in a flash.'

Joe waited all night by the telephone for word which never came. At dawn he borrowed a Tiger Moth and scoured the sea for fifteen miles out, but his only reward was the sight of white foam whipped by the wind from the heaving swell.

During the next week Teddy's place was taken by Flight Lieutenant Wagner, one of our more experienced pilots. In addition, Chris Hartley decided to spend a few days getting first-hand experience of the problem. He brought five more days of bad weather but managed to destroy a flying bomb on 15

July. For every bomb destroyed, each pilot probably shot at three or four, but they often had to break off as they approached the gun belt.

Then disaster struck the small detachment again. Wagner flew into the ground at high speed in poor visibility and killed himself (it was found later that Tempest altimeters all over-read at high speed near the ground, and the static vent was changed); Chris Hartley collided with a Mosquito as they both swooped on the same target at night. He managed to bale out and broke his ankle on landing; the Mosquito crew was killed.

There were sufficient collisions and near-misses, among the nightfighters engaged in anti-*Diver* operations, for pilots to start using navigation lights. This in turn attracted the Luftwaffe, who sent over intruders to profit from some easy pickings. When coupled with accidents caused by exceeding the aircraft flight envelopes, these losses started to assume significant proportions, but still the missiles came over.

Joe Berry was now alone; his personal score of bombs destroyed stood at twenty. It was obvious that the detachment's morale was in jeopardy and that something would have to be done; it was equally obvious that Joe would have to do it. He decided to play upon the rivalry shown between the day and night units. He chose a day when low cloud and rain made it hard to see from one side of the aerodrome to the other. As he hurried to his aircraft, head bent against the wind, he shot a quick glance at the day wing's Tempests. Dimly through the veil of rain and vapour could be seen the grey shapes snug behind their chocks; there would be no flying for them today, so he would do the job for them.

With a grunt of satisfaction he settled in his seat as the mechanic helped him on with his straps. Soon he had the hood wound forward and his cockpit check complete, then he was taking-off in a flurry of spray. Cloud base was only 400ft, but he broke clear of it again at 3,000ft. He called control; one bomb in the clear, just one, was all he wanted. And then suddenly there it was; streaking along among the cloud caps he made out the unfamiliar outline of a flying bomb in daylight. A short chase put him in position and he shot it down.

On his return to the rain-lashed airfield he could not resist the temptation to fly once, low and fast, across the mess tent. He landed without undue difficulty and taxied in. Grotesque figures in their dripping groundsheet capes—half-a-dozen airmen—came out to greet him. As he approached he could see that they were grinning broadly, despite the rain streaming off their faces. Three new pilots were posted in that day and one of them got his first kill that night; Joe got four. The crisis was over.

Berry was now detachment commander. He found that the calls upon his time were frequent, and he had to be in all places at all times if the little unit were to continue to function with its slender resources. When he did get to bed, sleep was constantly interrupted by the roar of the day wing taking-off as soon as it was light. The characteristic stutter of doodlebugs as they droned over Beachy Head was forever intruding into his dreams. But at least the weather had improved and the work went on.

On 23 July he shot down seven flying bombs in one night, as many as most people destroyed in the whole campaign. Once again he saw the blinding flash as a bomb blew up in his face at close range. Once again he flew through the violence of the subsiding debris, feeling the full force of the detonation. A fragment of bomb must have hit part of his aircraft, for he felt the shock as something exploded. The Tempest veered sharply. Automatically he corrected the movement, even as he flashed a comprehensive glance at the vital instruments. One of his fuel tanks was reading zero; it must have been holed. Fire in the air, the pilot's nightmare, obviously threatened; to make matters worse, his radio was dead.

Carefully descending through cloud over the sea, he flew until he recognised the coastline; from there it was easy. When he filled in his logbook next day, he wrote the following words:

'7 dest. Petrol tank exploded. R/T u/s.'

He did his best to explain to new pilots his method of range-finding. Their performance improved with experience, but Berry's score more than kept pace with their combined efforts. Next night the detachment's score topped the half hundred mark; Berry's personal score was 36½.

Unknown to him a battle was developing to obtain proper recognition for his feats. On 4 August his fellow pilots heard with delight that he had been awarded a bar to the DFC he had earned in the Mediterranean. He greeted the award by standing beer all round and then destroying five more bombs. Hartley, who had already put him up for the DSO, sent a hastener three days later when he reached his fifty and twice brought his damaged aircraft back without flaps or engine.

On 10 August came the news that he was promoted immediately to squadron leader to lead 501 Squadron flying Tempests at Manston. They were to turn over to *Diver*-hunting at night. On the first night he and his companions from Newchurch, who had all accompanied him, shot down eight bombs, while his new pilots got their hands in with some local night flying.

During the remainder of the month Berry found time to destroy seven *Divers*, but administration and training took up much of his time. The squadron buckled to its task with enthusiasm under his leadership; one pilot went so far as to tip three bombs up with his wing. At the end of the month Berry could look back on a squadron kill rate increased by tenfold since he had taken over; his own score stood at 60, top scorer by a long way—day or night.

Early in September the advancing Allied armies overran the V1 launching sites in the Pas de Calais area and the flow of bombs over the Channel slowed and stopped. Berry chafed at this sudden inactivity, until he decided to seek fresh targets on German airfields in Holland, now becoming crowded with aircraft retreating from France.

In the bleak hour before dawn on 1 October 1944, he and two other pilots walked out to their chilly aircraft. With luck they would catch the Luftwaffe napping before it was really light. The three Tempests took off in formation just after half-past five and headed out over the North Sea. The first streaks of light had started to paint the landscape as they arrived at the Dutch coast; they were 50ft up and going fast.

A solitary gun opened fire on their flank at full deflection, and Joe's aircraft was hit almost immediately. Before the horrified eyes of his companions it rolled onto its back and over the radio came his familiar voice with its last order, before the Tempest dived into the ground.

'Carry on, chaps. I've had it.'

A postscript appeared in the *London Gazette* nearly a year after the war ended. For 'courage and devotion to duty of a high order' Joe Berry was awarded a second bar to his DFC. Not many of his friends ever knew he got it; it probably gave him a laugh.

At this period 'Togs' Mellersh left us to return to a squadron. With 96, flying Mosquitos at West Malling, and now commanded by Edward Crew, he shot down no fewer than forty-two flying bombs at night, often using a borrowed Mustang. This was no mean feat when it is remembered that the VIs were so fast that the margin of speed was minimal. Mosquitos engaged in this anti-*Diver* role were usually the Mk XIX, low-level aircraft fitted with Merlin 25s. Exhaust-flame dampers were removed and the engines boosted to give + 24lb boost with 150 octane fuel. The nose sections had to be strengthened to withstand the effects of cannon fire at such high speeds. The usual system was for the Mosquito to patrol at about 8,000ft (2,000ft higher than Joe Berry in his faster Tempest had to go) if the weather were clear enough, so that it had 5,000–6,000ft advantage on the flying bomb; it could then increase speed in the dive and try to destroy its target before entering the AA gun belt. The guns by now were extremely lethal, for they were using proximity fuses which meant that any shells which passed near a solid object exploded as soon as they got close enough. So even a near miss could bring down an aircraft as easily as a flying bomb.

Deeply involved in the war against the V1 at the other end of the scale was the Assistant Chief of Air Staff (Intelligence), Air Vice-Marshal F. F. Inglis, CB, CBE. His had been the responsibility for co-ordination of reports and photo-cover of enemy research and development at Peenemünde and elsewhere; once the Germans started operations, he had to keep an eye on expansion of the launching sites and the subsequent incorporation of air-launched missiles. I, of course, did not know him at this time; still less did I know that his 13-year-old daughter would become my wife seven years later (and would doubtless have been horrified had she been presented to me in gym slip as my future bride).

27 June 1944

Flower *to Orléans and Châteaudun with AI Mk VIII. We get a contact en route to our target and this turns out to be a Liberator, who never knows that he has been looked at. Orléans/Bricy lights are on but no apparent activity, so we go on to Châteaudun. Contact at two miles and well above, so we climb from 2,000ft to 4,000ft and close to a visual on a JU 88. Open fire on his port engine for 2sec and bits fall away to the accompaniment of a small explosion, but he doesn't go up with a terrific bang as soon as I touch the gun button like so many combat reports you read. E/A* [enemy aircraft] *continues to fly straight and level, so we give him some more of the same with the same result. Next time I aim at the starboard engine but still he doesn't catch fire, so then I shoot at the port engine again. This time he starts burning and eventually pulls up over our heads so sharply that I worry lest he falls on top of us. As he hits the ground with a satisfactory splash of flame, I realise that the jinx is beaten and Mac and I shake hands just as though we are in an American movie.*

A second contact turns out to be another JU 88, but he sees us before we can attack. This is much to my astonishment because we are right underneath him in the very dark background of the earth and in the act of falling back to open fire; I wonder whether he has, perhaps, been warned from the ground that we are around. Anyway, he suddenly peels off, dives to ground level and gets away.

*On the way home we get yet another contact and close to a visual on an
unsuspecting Lancaster, who goes sedately on his way flying straight and
level and asking for trouble.*

Sometimes if I am up early and the sky is just right, I can live
again those early dawns as we returned from patrol in the first
pale light of day. It was early on a July day of 1944 when we
first saw it. The Allied armies were established on the Continent, Caen had been taken by Montgomery's troops and Bomber
Command was regularly striking at targets in France and
Germany, and Mac and I were on our way home from an
intruder. We had not had a particularly exciting night but were
full of proper content at a task completed—the enemy airfield
had been located and patrolled, and a train had shown up for
target practice at the outset of the journey home.

Crossing out near Ostende I had put a question.

'Shall we go in to Manston, Mac, or straight back to Wittering?'

'It'll mean another half an hour's flying,' he replied. I knew
what he was thinking: we had already been up for more than
four and a half hours which, in the cramped cockpit of the
Mosquito, was quite enough.

'Let's get it over straight away and get to bed,' I suggested.
My Scotsman, muttering something about his bottom, finally
agreed and so we shaped course for our own airfield. By now
the first red fingers of dawn were beginning to reach up to the
sky beyond the end of our starboard wing tip. We had left
Manston to port, crossed the coast at Orfordness and were
heading towards the Midlands.

Below us the sunlight was spilling and splashing into the
valleys already shrouded with morning mist, making it look as
though the countryside was filled with bubbling vapour. A
train was leaving a trail of white steam as it scuttled busily
along the track. Otherwise there was no movement. The world
slept.

It looked cold down there and somehow unreal, like a model.

'Look, Jerry.' Mac tapped me on the knee and pointed up to starboard. The morning sky, flecked with pink alto-cumulus, was being interlaced with vapour trails. One, two, three . . . nine, ten . . . twenty, thirty. The more I looked, the more I could count.

'They're Forts,' said Mac and I could make out the shape of some of the lower ones, silvery giants circling and climbing, climbing and circling, each starting its own vapour trail as soon as it was high enough. There must have been hundreds of them and they were an impressive demonstration of air power. There was something relentless and inevitable about the cold-blooded way they had been up before dawn preparing to blast Germany four or five hours later.

Down below, our swift Mosquito was creeping across the brown earth on its way home, its day just finished. Had the flying crews in the Fortresses been able to see into the cockpit of that Mosquito, they might perhaps have seen the pilot's lips move as he wished them luck. Nobody sang about a teeny-weeny bomb any more.

28 June 1944
Power cut this morning while I am shaving. As I use an electric razor, I have to go along to lunch half-shaved. But I have been caught this way before, so at least I am symmetrical while I shoot my line in the bar about last night's Hun.

Old habits die hard and I still shave today as though the electricity is about to fail: both sideburns first, then the moustache on each side followed by the middle chin, then both cheeks and finally the throat; it has still proved a useful procedure from time to time.

7 July 1944
Flower to airfields near Paris, with AI Mk X. Just before reaching the target area I am looking for a pinpoint when I see another aircraft out of the corner of my right eye. He is at the same level and just in front of our

starboard wing as he slowly converges; he crosses no more than 200ft ahead of us as we hold our breath. He must have been just outside the edge of our AI coverage, for Mac noticed nothing. I recognise him straight away as a JU 88 and Mac confirms this, so I let him draw away to 3,000ft while I get over the surprise and prepare for an attack. Mac gives the range from the AI, but I never lose sight of him in the bright moonlight. We come in from below and set fire to his port engine with our first burst of 2sec from 150yd. When I press the gun button again nothing happens except the whirr of the camera gun. I turn the safety switch and master switch off and on again, but we still take only pictures of him when I press the tit. Don't say we are going to lose this one through an electrical fault. Meanwhile one of the enemy crew is seen to bale out and he goes flying past our starboard wing tip. Eventually the guns decide to start up again and we stoke up a nice fire. The JU 88 has meanwhile headed for Coulommiers airfield, which has put on its lights with commendable promptness, but he pulls up and stalls into the ground about two miles west of the airfield.

9 July 1944
No trace of Teddy Daniel I'm afraid. Chris Hartley tells me I am to get the flight with rank of squadron leader.

I am informed that all four breech blocks on HK 360 (the Mosquito which gave us gun trouble over Coulommiers two nights ago) went forward as soon as the armourer pressed the button on the ground.

'Did you have the safety catch off, sir?'

This question is so stupid that it makes me angry. The next one is even more ridiculous.

'Did you press the gun button hard enough?'

If this is the best they can do we'll never win the war. I remain silent and show the bruises still evident on my thumb, where I had nearly pushed the tit through the stick. It is quite clear that nobody believes me, especially when the aircraft is taken over to the air firing range and fires all its ammunition faultlessly—not once but twice.

I fly the unit's Hornet Moth to Lichfield where Peter and Sheila have invited me to a party. He is now instructing at No 27 OTU [Operational Training Unit] and is back to flight lieutenant again. As I get

out of the aircraft, complete with two-and-a-half stripes for the first time,
he stares in disbelief.

'You'll be had up for impersonating a senior officer,' he says.

'Stand to attention and salute when you speak to an officer of field rank,'
I grin.

In the middle of the month one of the navigators of NFIU got
married near Ford, where he had been, of course, until we all
moved in April. We were all invited, so seven of us climbed
aboard our Coastal Command Wellington (appropriately
coloured white, we felt) and flew down for the occasion.
Lieutenant Peter Twiss, DSC, piloted and, on our arrival at
Ford, the duty flight was rather surprised to see not a battered
and weary Coastal Command crew emerge from the rigours of
the Battle of the Atlantic, but seven officers in their best RN
and RAF uniforms. We looked a bit more battered and weary
when we staggered back to the aircraft next day to fly home;
the party had been a successful one.

'At least,' I thought as we droned north, all gulping oxygen,
'$H2D$ has its uses. I'm glad they didn't take our word for it, and
make us keep the aeroplane.'

The Wellington was, in fact, withdrawn shortly after this and
our unfavourable report was accepted. It is interesting to note
how various schemes sometimes outstayed their operational
welcome according to the rhetoric of their protagonists. The
ultimate decisions were often made by politicians who were at
the mercy of any glib scientist who had access to the right
quarters. Here was a device which was proved useless almost on
its first flight but, although we gave it our usual methodical
and impartial treatment before writing a report, it was kept
at trials level long after it should have been relegated to the
history books. An even more vivid example of this flogging of
dead horses was the Turbinlite project about which I have
already written. I have never yet met any responsible aircrew
who could argue in favour of this circus, on which hundreds of
thousands of pounds and man hours were wasted. Somewhere

it had a loquacious sponsor who should have been made to fly in a nightfighter and then in a Turbinlite—in bad weather.

On 13 July the first example of *SN2* was captured by the Allies, when an inexperienced JU 88 crew landed at Wood-bridge in Suffolk, having misguidedly steered a reciprocal course. This enabled our scientists to get to work on a jammer and a homer. It also showed them that the Germans were alive to the fruits of homing on our transmissions, because the enemy nightfighter was full of electronic equipment, including a *Flensburg* homer. This was designed to enable the Germans to home onto Bomber Command's *Monica* tail-warning trans-missions.

Derek Jackson, now a wing commander, conducted flying trials in the JU 88 which proved conclusively to Air Marshal Harris that German nightfighters could home onto his bombers on their *Monica* transmissions alone. Harris's reaction was characteristic and immediate. He ordered the removal of *Monica* from all his aircraft and, alert at last to the dangers of too many transmissions, instructed his crews not to switch on their *H2S* until they were within enemy radar coverage, nor to use their IFF unless in distress. The stable door was now shut. In addition, Jackson was able to develop the correct *Window* to hinder this new German AI (a good radar operator, however, could usually work through such interference).

It is interesting to note that interrogation of Luftwaffe night-fighter pilots after the war revealed that they considered it more difficult to ply their trade on the eastern front than against the RAF. This was because the Russians had so little radio—and no radar—that it was not possible to home on their trans-missions as with Bomber Command. It seems incredible with hindsight that our aircraft could have been allowed to go on so long, not only advertising their presence in the air but, through test transmissions both from the ground and in the air during the day, giving warning of their intentions when there was to be an attack in the evening. The German interception service monitored our radio ground stations as W/T equipment was tested during the morning, noted increased aerial activity during the day as aircraft were tested in the air, picked up *H2S* transmissions from the bomber stream as soon as it left the English coast, and cross-checked this tracking by interrogating the bombers' IFF sets. Nightfighters took off and proceeded to trigger our IFF, home onto *H2S* and *Monica* transmissions and then make their interceptions with *SN2*, using *Lichtenstein* for the final stages if the former proved incapable of bringing the target near enough for the pilot to get a visual.

Attack was finally made from the relative invisibility and security of a position well below the target, by means of *Schräge Musik*, the upward-firing guns. It was scientific slaughter, largely made possible by the very aids which the authorities piled into the unsuspecting bombers. The luckless Lancasters, Halifaxes and Stirlings probably never knew half the time what hit them, yet they had the means of their own salvation had they but used it: the official corkscrew evasion was often enough to cause the Luftwaffe pilots to go searching for easier meat elsewhere; the extended corkscrew as developed by ourselves in conjunction with the Bomber Development Unit made final interception almost impossible; unfortunately it also made course-keeping difficult and so was never introduced as a means of evasion.

On 20 July 1944 the attempt was made to kill Hitler by means of a bomb planted underneath a table at a conference but, bearing in mind some of his decisions regarding the Luftwaffe, perhaps it was as well for us that he was spared.

Mac and I flew two more intruder trips before the end of July, both of which were uneventful. On the second our AI went u/s but, as we were otherwise serviceable, we pressed on in the hope of having the same sort of fortune as we did north of Paris when a JU 88 drifted in front of us. No such luck, however, but at least we did not drift in front of anyone else. Which set me wondering at the chances of our meeting that night. If the German had been 10sec later in his take-off—he only had to drop his map on the way out to his aircraft—we should have been the ones to drift in front of him.

Meanwhile we were also trying out *Monica* as a range indicator for flying bombs, to try to give a quick solution to this problem for aircraft attacking the bombs at night without AI (Mosquitos Mk VI and Tempests); a fair proportion of our effort was taken up with the Tempest detachment at Newchurch, being run by Joe Berry (who was not killed until October) and also the intruder effort, using Manston as a forward base, being run by myself. Low-priority trials were pushed into the background.

I see, however, from my logbook, that in four typical weeks at this time, apart from four intruder sorties, I flew four *Monica* flying-bomb warner tests in Mosquitos, sundry other trials including some in which the range of a target was automatically fed into the gyro gun sight from AI Mk X, a de-icer test for my naval colleagues on a Firefly, two trips to Newchurch in a Beaufighter to take mail and relief personnel to the Tempest detachment, a test of GCF as it was called at first (Ground Controlled Flying), but later came to be known as GCA (Ground Controlled Approach, or blind landing by radar control) in a Typhoon, several acceptance checks on new Tempests for the Newchurch detachment, a trip to Halton in the unit's Hornet Moth to take an airman on leave, and delivery of a Firefly to Lee-on-Solent to collect another Firefly for NFIU, who were short of pilots and couldn't do it for themselves.

8 INTRUDER SORTIE

It might be of interest at this point to include the sequence of events of a typical intruder operation as seen, not only from the cockpit, but also from the ground.

Hopefully we would test our aeroplane in the morning or early afternoon and then bother the groundcrew until every little thing was on the top line. There would always be the debate as to whether, if the AI were not 100 per cent efficient, it was worth the risk of the special signals section tuning it up to get, perhaps, a better maximum range and thus spoiling the minimum range in the process. Better the devil you know than the devil you don't was the usual verdict. The duty navigator would be constantly bothered for the target and details of the bomber effort until finally, perhaps at tea time, one of us would be called away to the telephone.

'Howard-Williams here.'

'Oh, Jerry, this is Jimmy here. I've got the target.'

'Where is it?'

'Well, you've been there before. The set-up looks good. I'll give you the gen if you come up to the aerodrome.'

I would go dashing back to the dining-room to haul Mac away from the remains of his tea, and we'd both rush up to the aerodrome.

In dispersal the duty navigator would already have the bomber target marked, together with the route. The RCM screens and any spoofs would be shown and, most important, our own aerodrome target, time of the bomber raid and our own patrol times. FIU had a high reputation for reaching their target, so we usually had a good draw.

'Let's see. Bomber prang at 12.05 and we're on target from one until two. We ought to be in a good position to catch them landing back.'

'Do you think we can do it from here, or had we better refuel at Manston?'

'It's only about 400 miles there. We ought to be quite OK. I'll get onto met, if you start working out a few tracks from the flak map.'

A careful study of this map was always made, so as to avoid the areas of flak concentration and the searchlight belts as much as possible.

For the next hour and a half the dispersal would be a busy place. Flak maps, met officer, tracks, winds, courses, messages to the groundcrew about filling the drop tanks and when to come on duty, checking the track on the flak map, checking the courses, memorising the appearance of main pin-points—all these matters would be muddled up. From this chaos would emerge, some time before dinner, a crew who knew that their aircraft was ready, that they were going to a good target the best way, and that everything that could be done on the ground had been done. Then a call at station intelligence on the way back to the mess for the gen card giving all the colours of the day—and so to dinner.

After dinner we would go to our rooms to dress for the trip. All normal items had to be emptied from our pockets in case they gave away information if we were captured—even a bus ticket could help an interrogator by supplying a date and a place for him to work on. I always carried my five-shilling piece and my silk scarf as talismans.

We had a special pack with escape aids such as compass, maps and money which we drew from the intelligence section. This would, of course, have been confiscated as soon as we were first captured, but we also had several compasses hidden about our persons where it was hoped they would escape detection by the Germans, and so could be kept for later use, possibly from prisoner-of-war camp. These were constantly changing as their

132

secrets were discovered, but I still possess the small brass crested shoulder button which unscrewed (clockwise) to reveal a compass, and a collar stud from whose base paint could be scraped to show a magnetic needle. There were also two rough metal flybuttons of the kind used on service battledress trousers, which could be cut off and balanced one on the other to give a compass bearing.

A sheath knife stuck down my flying boot and a torch with a red paper screen to filter the light completed my preparations.

Back in dispersal again and a quick check would be made to see that the correct colours were in the aeroplane. A final call to operations to see if they had any more information and the time would come for take-off.

In radio silence the aircraft would pick its way round the aerodrome to the end of the runway, where it would get a green light after flashing the letter of the period on its recognition light. Check that the propellers are in fine pitch, the petrol tanks full and on outers, glycol temperatures below 100°C, throttle nut tight, flaps up or 10° according to load, radiator flaps open and gyro set. Onto the runway switch off the navigation lights and open with the throttles, the port one a little in advance of the other to correct the swing with all that petrol aboard. Stick slightly forward to get the tail up, and the end of the runway would start to rush nearer. As the Mosquito was invariably so heavily laden, it would have to be almost pulled off the ground. A quick change-over from visual to instrument flying, swap hands on the stick and whip up the wheels—'Hold the lever up, Mac'—and then left hand back to the throttles while the right took over the stick again. Keep the climb and dive needle just above the zero mark and, when the speed reached 180mph (single-engine speed), throttle back to + 7lb boost and 2,650rpm. Climb smartly away to port and, after checking the directional gyro on the Pole Star (010 degrees magnetic), set course over the airfield, whose lights could be seen below.

'OK, Mac. Setting course. Go over to inners. Oxygen at

15,000ft.' Mac would make his second entry in the rough log he kept on his knee pad. He would then switch on the oxygen so that it flowed at the rate suitable for flying at 15,000ft. Although we would be operating well below oxygen height, its use helped night vision and it was as well to have it flowing in case we had a chase up to high altitude and forgot it in the excitement.

Climbing away to 2,000ft or 3,000ft Mac would try the AI and *Gee*. A few grunts as he bent forward to peer into the visor, or twisted round to the *Gee* behind my shoulder, would not tell me anything.

'All OK?'

'Yes, they look all right. I'm just taking a fix.'

'Course was 073° wasn't it?'

'Just a minute . . . yes, 073°.'

Periods of silence now would be punctuated by such remarks as:

'How long on this leg?'

'How long before we get to the coast?'

'Are we on track?' All these from me.

'What are you steering?'

'Can you see anything about half a mile ahead and 10° up?'

'We're a bit to port of track. Leave it though, we'll get another fix from *Gee* in a few minutes and we'll see where that puts us.' All from Mac.

The sortie really only began when we crossed the English coast on the way out. This would give us a pinpoint from which to start and down we would go to 500ft or less, to keep out of the enemy's radar cover as long as possible over the North Sea. Frequent checks on *Gee* and minor alterations of course would take up all our time over this part of the route, as we checked on the forecast wind and recalculated it. It was important to cross the enemy coast at the right place, mainly to avoid being shot at too much.

'You should be seeing the coast soon.'

'I think I can.' Sometimes this was a false alarm, caused by a patch of low-lying cloud darker than the rest, but eventually out of the hazy horizon would emerge something more solid.

There were several places on the coastline where anti-aircraft and radar defences left slight gaps, and we would plan our route to use one of these: Point d'Ailly near Dieppe and Egmond on the Dutch coast were two favourites. Half way through the sea crossing Mac would work out whether we needed to alter course to hit the crossing-in point spot on and I would make the necessary correction. As we neared the coast we dropped lower and lower, until we were flying at no more than 200ft above the water, which usually showed grey with white foam flecking the wave tops below us in the gloom. In low cloud or rain I would have to force myself to push the Mosquito down lower still, so that we could stay in sight of the surface.

About seven or eight miles (or two minutes) short of the coast I would open the throttles to + 6lb boost and 2,650rpm and pull the aircraft up to 3,500–4,000ft so as to avoid small-arms fire. We usually crossed in with a shallow snaking dive down to 1,000ft again, by which time we would be going fast enough to take most gun positions by surprise. Never once on any of our trips were we shot at as we actually crossed the coast on the way in. When I read after the war that the Dambusters had lost no less than seven aircraft out of eighteen on the way to the Ruhr dams on their epic raid (they only lost two while actually over the target, where flak could have been expected to be at its worst), it made me sad to think that Bomber Command cannot have sought advice from Fighter Command as to the best method of flying a low-level sortie, or they would never have tried it quite the way they did.

Once over enemy territory we stayed as low as the surrounding hills and weather would allow. The German radar stations could by now be heard interfering on the R/T every time the beam swept round onto us. Right down to as low as we dared and, with luck, the interference would stop, thus making us think that we had shaken off the probing finger of radar pulses. Now we could shape our course for the next pin-point and the conversation would centre round how *Gee* was faring through the jamming. Sooner or later, usually sooner low down, we would give it up and resort to such map-reading as we could: rivers and lakes (all so much bigger in France and Germany than in England), sometimes railways, roads and woods on a moonlit night, would help us on our way. Even the German aerial flashing beacons were useful, because we would use those on the way home that we had spotted and noted on the outward journey.

In clear weather we could map read from pin-point to pin-point; when the clouds came down and it rained we would stay below as long as we knew exactly where we were or while there was ample margin but, as soon as we were in doubt as to our position or there was less than 500ft clearance between the ground and the clouds, we would go up through it. The decision was always postponed as long as possible because it meant that, sooner or later, we would have to come down again not knowing where we were or how low the cloud base was. Study of the map and estimation of our reckoned position would show us the probable height of the ground beneath us; down we would come gingerly, hoping for a break in the cloud to show us the ground below—there were usually lights of some kind to be seen: aerial beacons, railway signals, factory furnaces or even cars on the roads. If it were stormy, then we just had to ride it out as I held on to the control column more firmly, ignoring the static discharge criss-crossing the windscreen with miniature light-ning flashes. Once below cloud would come the task of finding exactly where we were, in which the pilot perforce played a large part because the navigator had to keep checking on the AI and *Monica* in case any enemy aircraft were about. The dull red glow of screened torches would light the cockpit from time to time as we pored over the map, trying to reconcile what we could see of the ground with where we thought we should be on the map.

One memory stands out. We were flying fast and low across France on our way to some German aerodrome and we approached the French town of Lens. Suddenly, ahead of us, I saw a door open at the front of a house and the light shone through from inside. A woman ran down the steps and waved as she ran. For a brief moment she was thrown into sharp relief against the yellow light behind her, forming a silhouette which burned itself into my brain; then we were gone. She had obviously run a considerable risk in breaking black-out regulations, but she created a warm glow in the Mosquito cockpit which lasted throughout our trip, indeed which can still be felt after more than a quarter of a century.

Meanwhile, back at dispersal the air outside the hut is cold and dark, for it is a winter's night. A telephone orderly is stretched out in an easy chair in front of the stove and around him, scattered on the floor where he has cast them, are various periodicals: *Picture Post, Aircraft Recognition, Tee Emm, Men Only* and several others. Lights are still burning over the navigation benches, the wireless is switched on but no sound comes from it as it is well after midnight. Recognition models of German aircraft hang on pieces of black cotton from the ceiling.

The orderly sleeps; he is waiting. Somewhere in the night, if all is well, two Mosquitos are on their way home from Germany.

Brrr Brrr. Brrr Brrr. A bell quietly insinuates itself into the orderly's mind. He wakes, gets up and crosses the room to the telephone.

'FIU dispersal.'

'Flying control here,' says the receiver. 'Squadron Leader Howard-Williams has just contacted us on the R/T. He should be landing in about a quarter of an hour.'

'OK sir, thank you.' He goes to the kettle standing on the table and places it on the fire. He then rings up the groundcrew to tell them to expect the first aircraft in about ten minutes. A few minutes later flying control tells him that the second machine is also on its way.

Soon the unmistakable sound of a Mosquito is heard in the circuit. After a while the squeal of the touch-down is followed by the gentle rumble of idling engines. The whine of brakes is then interrupted by bursts of engine as the aeroplane slowly picks its way round the dimly lit perimeter track. It evidently reaches its dispersal point, for the engines are run for a few seconds to clear the plugs and one after the other are choked into silence. All is quiet again. Gradually the pilot and his navigator can be heard approaching the hut. They come through the door, blinking in the strong light.

'Evening, Tomkins, or good morning, rather. Got any tea for us?'

Two faces, lined with sweat and the marks of helmets and oxygen masks, look expectantly at the orderly. But he is already coming towards them with a pint mug of tea in each hand. Tea made in the way that he knows best: not so hot as to prevent immediate drinking, but not tepid; it is sweet too, so as to re-place energy used up as well as moisture. And the kettle is standing by, ready to refill the pot as long as it is required.

'Thank you, Tomkins. This is exactly it.'

That is his only reward for sitting up for four or five hours, waiting, waiting. He does not ask for more, happy in the knowledge that they also serve . . . Once his cup was filled when the pilot said:

'The train had stopped and I was just climbing away, when I came round again and gave it one more burst. That's for Tomkins, I said. It was a bloody good shot too.'

Meanwhile the second Mosquito has been heard coming in. Over their tea the two pilots get together and so do the two navigators.

'Have any luck?'

'Got a train east of . . .'

'. . . trouble with the eastern chain earlier than usual.'

'. . . no flak until . . .'

'Did you try the Ruhr chain? I did and . . .'

'. . . good weather up to the Rhine, then . . .'

'. . . they were obviously landing, but where they were holding [waiting permission to land], God only knows.'

By now everyone is stretched out in armchairs. Mae Wests, helmets, gloves and maps are strewn round the room. There is a pleasant untidiness about the place and the crews are luxuriating in it. And they keep coming back for more of that hot sweet tea, which can only ever be truly appreciated by those who have tasted it under these special circumstances. When they have unwound their nervous systems they rise, stretch and collect their belongings. Pausing at the door they turn to thank the orderly and then make for the intelligence section to write their reports, and so to a bacon-and-egg night-flying supper in the mess, followed by bed.

Back in dispersal the orderly gets down to some washing up.

11 August 1944
Intruder to airfields in the Paris area. No activity but, on our way home, we are feeling frustrated and aggressive so we shoot up a searchlight which tries to engage us. Then we see a car speeding along a road, its rather dim headlights from time to time reinforced by a vast probing spotlight which lights up the road for a great distance. On the principle that this can only belong to a Very Important German, we deliver an attack on it, which results in the immediate extinction of all his lights and he winds up in small pieces.

14 August 1944
To Farnborough in a Beaufighter with Bill Bailey to collect a Messerschmitt 410 for night-flying trials. This aircraft was captured in Italy, we are led to believe. It is the photographic version, with twin barbette turrets still installed and some expensive cameras. Roly Falk of RAE [Wing Commander R. J. Falk, OBE, AFC, Chief Test Pilot of the Royal Aircraft Establishment. In passing it is of interest to note the coincidence that the commanding officer of the Luftwaffe's first nightfighter Geschwader was called Falck] *shows me the tits and Bill waits for me so that he can fly escort on the way back.*

The 410 is nothing spectacular. More like a Beau to handle than a Mossie, but then we are spoiled by the smoothness of the latter.

20 August 1944
We return to Ford today! Great rejoicing. As flight commander, I have

pick of the aircraft to take down and choose the Mustang III which has just been delivered for night-flying trials. This proves to be an exciting aeroplane: fast, easy to fly and with, of course, an incredible duration. We go in an enormous Balbo [kind of formation], *and are glad to be back. We shall have to return tomorrow to make another formation delivery, because we have about twice as many aeroplanes as pilots.*

That night we sing our hymn in the mess with great fervour. To the obvious tune we bellow:

> *Hark my soul it is the Lord,*
> *Coming in to land at Ford,*
> *Listening out on channel C*
> *Singing: Honey have a sniff have a sniff on me.*

31 August 1944
Intruder again. We still have to go to Manston to refuel as this adds about an hour to our endurance. This time Denis Lake comes with me, as Mac is sick. Bill Maguire and Taffy Jones are also with us tonight. We get to Manston in good time and, as we are not off until midnight, we all go to a cinema in Margate. Bill is a bluff, hearty character with a big moustache, who has come to us from John Cunningham in 85 Squadron. Not for the first time I wonder how people can solemnly go to a film and take in any of it, knowing that in three or four hours they may be dead. But I go along to show that I'm as nonchalant as they are and sit through it fretting about the trip, this time a freelance with AI Mk VIII across the breadth of Germany, calling at as many nightfighter airfields as we care to visit. There is no bomber prang tonight so we shall be lucky to find any Huns flying. It is my thirteenth offensive trip and I try to remember that thirteen is my lucky number as I was born on that date.

We have a five-hour trip and find nine airfields in the moonlight. Some of them are not lit, but ability in low-level fast navigation comes with practice and we find them all, so beat up the unlit ones just to show the Hun that we can still find him even when he doesn't put his lights on. We strafe a train on the way home and bits start coming off the front of the Mosquito. It makes a hell of a noise and for a moment I think we have been hit by the return fire.

3 September 1944
This lot's been going five years now; and they used to boast about the
length of the 1914–18 war! Apparently RAF/WAAF relationships
reached an all-time low while we were away, so Fighter Command (Air
Defence of Great Britain, I beg their pardons) posted in a new Queen
Bee to smooth things over. I must say, she's rather a poppet and I can't
imagine poor relationships where she's around.

7 September 1944
First solo on the Spitfire at last! This is a Mk IX and it is all it's
cracked up to be: smooth, fast and manoeuvrable.

9 September 1944
AI Mk X Flower *to Rheine, Twente and Plantelünne in north-west*
Germany. Excellent visibility and we have no trouble in navigation. No
activity but we stray too near Rheine and get caught in the 'whirling
spray'. This is the name we have given to one gun or battery of guns,
to the west of the airfield which we have seen several times in action. It fires
a lot of tracer, and hosepipes the air all round its target with a remarkable
effect. It must be very inefficient, but it is impressive and we are glad to
get out of it. After we are clear, we call up on the R/T to Peter Twiss
who is in the vicinity and merely say: 'Phew!' He laughs.

11 September 1944
Swanning [pleasure trip] *to Vannes in France. We go pubbing and*
chat to the French. After spending the night with the USAAF we fly
home next day.

16 September 1944
Air Defence of Great Britain yesterday went back to being called Fighter
Command—and a damn good thing too.
    Flower to Gütersloh and Paderborn in HK 360. We find we are
straying well north of track over the North Sea, so correct two or three
times before having to turn south and fly for five minutes to get back to the
right place. We are keen to establish the correct wind before we cross in,
because we shall not have the use of Gee *much after that.*

I have brought a bottle of milk with me because Denis Lake always does this and says it is a great reviver. We are flying at 500ft still over the North Sea and all is smooth, so I decide to drink my milk. No sooner have I got the top off and taken a swig than we find ourselves over a convoy. Friend or foe makes no difference and everything opens up at us, so we need to take avoiding action. Instead of dropping the bottle on the floor and throwing the Mosquito round the sky, my first thought is not to spill any milk, so I look round for somewhere to put it.

'Oh, for God's sake, give it to me,' says Mac grabbing for it. 'Now get on and earn your living, driver.'

As we cross in just north of the Hague, we see a white flame pulsing at ground level and, because nobody has told us that V2s don't take-off with a rush like a child's firework rocket, we don't realise what we are looking at. They have only been coming over for about a week and are still rather strange and secret. A pity, because we were in a perfect position to have a shot at it and it would have been nice to be able to say that we had shot down a V2, not to mention the saving of life in England.

After leaving the Zuider Zee we get hopelessly lost. We can't even find the Dümmer See, which is saying something. So we cruise round for three hours freelancing in a confined space so as not to get too lost and then go home—which isn't easy as the compass seems to be haywire. Beat up a train on the way.

17 September 1944
As I walk into the mess at lunchtime, still rubbing the sleep out of my eyes, Barbara, our new Queen Bee, asks me if I had a good trip. She had happened to be around last night when Mac and I left the mess to go down to dispersal for take-off, so she knew we were out. I make a conventional reply and forebear to add that I reckon we had a special prayer looking after us, but I had a definite feeling all evening.

We tried everything to discover what was wrong with that compass. It seemed to be a progressive problem, which built up during the flight. But we failed to find the fault until I suggested that we turn on the cockpit lighting, even though we were testing by day; this was the only factor left which reproduced the conditions of failure and it had to be the reason. And so it turned out. Somewhere in the lighting circuit there was a magnetic influence affecting the compass, so we ripped out the ultra-violet lighting and rewired it.

But HK 360 wasn't finished with us yet. About two weeks later Bill Maguire and Taffy Jones took the aircraft to Twente airfield and were spot on with their luck. They arrived just as about two dozen German nightfighters were landing back after a raid by Bomber Command. Taffy could also 'see' further aircraft at extreme range each time they circled towards the nearby airfield of Rheine; obviously the same was going on there. They closed one contact to visual and there was a nice fat JU 88. On pulling up to shoot it down—nothing! Only the camera gun was working, just as it had with Mac and me at Coulommiers. They tried everything but never got a single shot fired. So they went right in close and drew pictures of the Hun's radar antennae, just in case it would help, and then peeled off disgustedly and came home.

Next day all four breech blocks flew forward as soon as the armourer pressed the gun button.

I may say that I watched all this with a certain amount of sympathetic interest. It must have been about as maddening as possible for Bill, but at least it showed that I hadn't been imagining things. We never found the cause, but pulled every bit of electrical wiring out of that aircraft and rewired it from scratch.

29 September 1944
Air Marshal Hill, the C-in-C Fighter Command, has to go to Paris for a conference; Group Captain Hiscox, Night Ops, is going with him. Chris Hartley takes the air marshal in a Mosquito and I take Hicko in a Beau. The weather is lousy and we soon lose sight of one another in low cloud, so Chris radios instructions to return to Northolt. There is then much discussion out of my hearing, and the upshot is that both the C-in-C and Hicko climb into my Beaufighter and we set off again. Fortunately, I have done my homework on the route and wasn't relying on formating on

the CO, so my maps are properly marked with tracks and easily identified turning points. The Beau is super for bad-weather flying, as the
visibility from the cockpit is good and the clear-vision panels really work.
We reach Buc, just outside Paris, in just over an hour and I have three
hours to kill, which is pleasant. The weather has got worse, if anything,
for the return trip and cloud base at the south coast is down to 500ft with
visibility not much more than a couple of miles. I am very much aware
that we can easily be mistaken for a JU 88 approaching head on out of
the gloom and, my important passengers apart, I do not want to be shot
up or shot down by some trigger-happy gunner keen to show his accuracy.
There has been a spate of this sort of mix-up in identification recently
and fortunately somebody has established a drill for just these circumstances. I wait until we are a mile from the coast and then turn parallel
with it and lower my undercarriage.

'Hello, Hunchback, hello, Hunchback,' I call on sector-control
frequency. 'This is Hedon 37 about one mile south of Littlehampton and
identifying. Hedon 37 identifying. Over.'

After flying for about a minute broadside on with wheels down, so
that even the stupidest gunner (and he's the one this particular pantomime
is being staged for) can see that we are friendly, I turn towards the coast
again, raise the wheels and we cross in. It works and we are unmolested.

30 September 1944
Comparative speed trials of ME 410 with a Mosquito XVII; the
Mossie wins. Then an NFT and an intruder to Münster. The Hun has
taken to launching flying bombs from HE 111s, since so many of the
launching sites in France have been overrun. We are searching for these
aircraft landing back after a sortie. No activity but we have a low-level
AI chase at 280mph on the way home, which we soon recognise as friendly
by means of his infra-red identification [coded lights which could
only be picked up by an infra-red telescope mounted above the
dashboard]. We guess that it will be another Mosquito going home
and, as it doesn't take us out of our way, we close to a visual. It is indeed
a Mossie and I can't resist the temptation to give him a fright. I transmit
the standard interrogation for doubtful circumstances on our common
frequency (channel C, command guard, 121·5 mc/s):

'*Bogey, bogey, waggle your wings.*'

This must sound very loud and close to him, as indeed it is, and has the desired effect of causing him to rear up like a startled jack rabbit and waggle his wings frantically in a most satisfactory manner.

'*OK, OK,*' I call and pull up alongside him. We fly together for a while and then I peel off. On landing at Manston to refuel, I find our friend there and he is from 605, one of the intruder squadrons without AI. We pull his leg about being asleep on the job.

16 October 1944

Our name has changed from Fighter Interception Unit to Fighter Interception Development Squadron. We are now part of a mammoth empire called the Central Fighter Establishment and we think that FIDS doesn't sound half as nice as FIU. The day boys, centred on the Air Fighting Development Unit and the Fighter Leaders School, will be at Tangmere and we shall be at Ford, joining with the Navigator Radio Leaders School to start the Night Fighter Development Wing. Jobs for the boys as far as I can see, because we shall go on as before but there will be an air commodore and a group captain around now.

19 October 1944

First solo on a Grumman Hellcat, which the navy have got at NFIU (they keep their original title, as they don't see why our reorganisation has to affect them. Sensible people). The Hellcat tests are connected with a Monica-*style* rear warner. Then an NFT in a Mosquito followed by an intruder to Stuttgart. An early take-off for a change, so we should get back home to bed at a reasonable hour. For the first time on one of these trips I have to pee into the little rubber bottle they give you. It's a hell of a game getting it all sorted out but I make it in the end, only for Mac to spill the bloody thing putting it away. This goes over the rice paper gen card, which gives the colours of the day (both British and German), but we can still just read it. It then freezes in the sub-zero temperature of the bottom of the cockpit floor, where it has been relegated as Mac won't put it in his pocket.

'Who eats the rice paper if we are shot down, Mac?' I ask. 'You because you spilled the pee on it, or me because it's mine?'

We reach Stuttgart at quarter-past ten for an hour's patrol and aircraft are obviously landing, but they have got it well buttoned up and Mac can't get a contact anywhere. There is a layer of cloud at 2,000ft and we fly below it and above it, searching for their holding area or even their approach lane, but have no luck. We are just thinking of setting course for home, when a landing lamp goes on for a couple of seconds, about a mile out and 200ft up; it is repeated about fifteen seconds later at half a mile. At neither of these times were we in a position to attack, being about two miles away from the runway when the light first came on.

'He's bound to switch it on again at touch-down,' I say to Mac and start a dive at the beginning of the runway, hoping to time it right. Mac calls out the height.

We are getting very low and close and I begin to think that our Hun is too wily when, sure enough, the light comes on again at the beginning of the runway, right where we are going. I just have time to line up my sights and give him a 1sec burst before we are over and past him. We see strikes round the light, which goes out immediately, but there is no fire. We fly across the camp at about 50ft and so away. Some searchlights and light flak later engage us without any result and we fly off home.

When we get home at two o'clock in the morning after stopping at Manston to refuel, George Jones and Bernard Lush are already in dispersal and they too have had a frustrating evening. They got a visual on a JU 88, only to find that their gunsight was u/s. George hosepiped around his target but all he managed was to scare his Hun away with a few dents in him.

George Jones was a prematurely balding young man of precise character, who never jumped to conclusions but preferred to weigh all problems with a certain amount of deliberation. His navigator Bernard Lush was, like Mac, a large man and, again like Mac, somewhat over the average age for flying. He suffered from spine trouble, which was not the best of problems to bring to the cramped cockpit of the Mosquito, but he was a tough character and refused to complain or to let it affect his flying on operations. It is a measure of how we judged a man in those days that it was a year before I realised that Bernard was a practising Jew, and it only registered then because somebody wondered whether he would get 'special treatment' from the Germans if he were shot down and made prisoner. His disability got slowly worse until, towards the end of the war, he had to force his huge frame into the small entrance hatch of the Mosquito and, at the end of a four- or five-hour flight, he was practically seized in the doubled-up position required for bending over the AI set. He could have got off flying on medical grounds but there is none so tough as a tough Jew, and Bernard never gave up.

19 October 1944 (continued)
I am busy relating our own fun and games, with suitable epithets and embellishments (particularly when it comes to the spilling of the pee bottle on the gen card) when I slowly become aware of a stranger sitting in a chair in the corner. He is wearing a rather scruffy dark blue reefer jacket so, because this garment has no badges of rank, I can't tell what or who he is. I continue with my story and, when I have finished, he comes across to introduce himself. It is the new AOC of the Central Fighter Establishment, come to see for himself how the night wing works: Air Commodore 'Batchy' Atcherly [later Air Chief Marshal Sir Richard Atcherly, KBE, CB, AFC], *whom I last saw two-and-a-half years ago with John Cunningham at Fairwood Common. George Jones, having himself been caught unawares by the AOC's incognito presence, didn't see why we should be warned, so he let us rant on unchecked while the air commodore sat there drinking it all in. He is, of course, an aircrew's commander and has a reputation for standing up for his men in all reasonable—and many unreasonable—situations. Quite obviously he wants to find out for himself how the operational half of his empire gets along at the sharp end, for he wouldn't wait up until two o'clock in the morning just to pass the time of day. When we have got over our embarrassment, Mac and I have a talk with our new AOC and he proves very human. We are glad that there has been some activity to report, because we in the night wing are very conscious of the fact that the day-wing development units don't carry their experiments to the enemy as we do; and we keep reminding them of this.*

147

The Heinkel 111s which were launching V1s over the North Sea gave the Mosquitos charged with the task of intercepting them a certain amount of trouble, funnily enough because the Mosquitos were too fast. Luftwaffe tactics were to come across the North Sea at about 50–100ft so as to keep under our coastal radar coverage, then climb to 1,500ft and open up to minimum launching speed (150mph), release their bomb and turn and dive away again to just above the water. There were about seven minutes from the time the HE 111 started climbing, and so showed on the British shore radar, until it dived for the surface again, so interceptions had to be quick. While it was climbing, the launching aircraft was doing only 110mph at which speed Mosquitos fell out of the sky. So somebody in Fighter Command suggested bringing Beaufighters out of retirement for the job, since they had a much lower stalling speed than the Mosquito. FIDS already had several Beaufighters with AI Mk VIII (we had even had one with AI Mk X at one time) in an operational condition, so we were naturals for trials. On 26 October Mac and I flew to Coltishall to join 125 Squadron, the resident Mosquitos, on the night's readiness programme. There was no activity.

The following night I flew a Firefly for the navy on *ASH* trials, then Mac and I went on another intruder to the Stuttgart area. There was no aerial activity, but the German railways seemed to be busy that night. Starting at the Strasbourg marshalling yards, we fired at a total of six trains on the way home.

Marshalling yards were interesting targets, sometimes bristling with light and heavy AA guns, and also apt to be protected by balloons on occasions. If the defences were on the ball they could give a most unfriendly reception, so these were not exactly safe spots, even for one low-level run; we usually didn't ask for trouble by making a second pass unless there was a particularly tempting target—a classification which, I am glad to say, was hard to discern at night.

Circling Strasbourg, I could feel my heart thumping in my

chest as I switched off the safety catch and selected my line of approach. With tightening stomach I pushed the stick forward to lower the nose and then swung into the attack, bracing my feet firmly on the rudder bar, so as to be able to bring the gun-sight to bear as soon as a suitable aiming point should appear. The familiar feeling of exhilaration gripped me as we were borne inexorably down to the target. The first glowing tracer bullets of the reception committee curled their way lazily up towards us out of the darkness, and caused a surge of excitement to sweep through me. There was no turning back now and nothing could alter the course of the next few seconds. Return fire was coming from all sides by now, and the coloured balls of fire, seemingly so slow as they started their journey, suddenly started whipping past the cockpit. The outline of a large engine detached itself from the confusion of darkness and shadow on the ground. I sighted quickly on the stationary target and pressed the gun button on the spade grip of the control column, all thought of return fire forgotten. Our four 20mm cannons crashed solidly under us and flashes appeared on the engine's steel casing as our explosive shells struck home; the light from these strikes revealed that we were also hitting some rolling stock on the near side of the target.

Then Mac reminded me that we were down to about 50ft, so I pulled up and away. Return fire chased us into the night, but there was nothing to make us go back for more; we flew off into the tranquil darkness in a sense of anti-climax.

My custom when attacking trains was always to aim for the engine for two reasons: first if it were moving one never knew who was in the train—it could be women and children, prisoners of war, detainees or other non-combatant categories; secondly, engines were presumably more valuable to the Germans than railway carriages. That night we got a satisfactory explosion of steam after one of our later attacks, and on our sixth and final train we were getting near to the front line again so we decided to finish our ammunition; we accordingly made five runs at the wretched target as it lay stationary between some trees, so we considered that the Germans wouldn't have got much more use out of that particular engine.

During the course of our journey home we strayed from track on one occasion—unusual for us—and suddenly found ourselves being coned by searchlights and shot at by a lot of flak.

'It must be Cologne,' said Mac.

'Which way do I turn?' I asked, my head well inside the cockpit away from the brilliant glare of blinding light outside. 'And make sure you send us the right way, because there are a lot of balloons here.'

'Turn left,' replied Mac. 'I know about the balloons, I can see them down below us.'

'Christ, so they are.' I hauled the aircraft hard round and briefly glimpsed there below us, close to the ground, the gas-bags gleaming dully in the reflections from the searchlights. I buried my nose in the cockpit again, thanked the Lord that the Germans hadn't decided to send up their balloon barrage that night, and blessed the practice at flying in searchlights at low altitude that I had received doing canopy and co-op exercises with our own searchlights in England.

It looked to me for all the world as if Mac were taking us straight over the built-up area, but he had the map and it was no good asking for directions and then not taking them. He was right, of course, and we were out of danger in a few minutes without being hit.

When I was stationed with the RAF in Germany in 1953, I was buying paint in a shop in Cologne one day and got to swapping war experiences with the friendly German behind the counter.

'What was your job, then?' I asked, having told him mine.

'I was on anti-aircraft guns at Cologne,' he replied.

'Well, you missed me,' I grinned.

2 November 1944
Flower to Bonn airfield with a Mosquito XIX and AI Mk X. Don Spurgeon comes with me as Mac is away on other duty. We find ropey

weather in the target area with low cloud and haze. It is enough to keep the Hun on the ground and is too much for train busting.

Flight Lieutenant E. Hedgcoe and Flying Officer N. Bamford went for ten days' detachment to 100 Group at Swannington about now. They had a fruitful stay, shooting down three ME 110s and a JU 88 in three trips. On their return to the unit, they were able to get us up to date on 100 Group's operations and some of their problems and requirements. *Perfectos* which, it will be remembered, was the device designed to home onto German IFF equipment, and on which we had done a lot of the early trials, was at last coming into squadron service with 100 Group and we were keen to know how it was getting on.

4 November 1944
Mac and I take a Beau with AI Mk VIII to Coltishall again. This time Hopton CHEL [Chain Home, Extra Low-looking coastal defence radar station] *gives us trade at 1,500ft, crossing port to starboard but say they can give no more help. I point the Beau to port a bit and Mac soon gets a contact at 1½ miles. We let it cross us and I lower 30° of flap for the approach. We close to a visual quickly and it is a Heinkel 111 going west at 140mph, looking for all the world like a sinister black crow as it prepares to release its flying bomb from underneath the right wing. I am fed up with firing 1sec bursts at port or starboard engines and then waiting for the immediate explosion which only seems to occur in other people's combat reports. Nobody's going to survive a ditching in the North Sea for long tonight anyway, so I take aim on the centre of the Hun's fuselage and hold my thumb on the gun button. Things start happening immediately; a nice big fire breaks out and he nosedives straight into the drink, complete with flying bomb, where a pool of burning fuel spreads briefly on the surface sending flames dancing on the water.*
   'Hello, Arcade, 37 here. Thanks for your help, that one's burning nicely. Fix please. Any more trade? 37 over.'
   'Well done 37. We can't help you any more, but there are still signs of activity in your area. Your pigeons are 315 sixty miles. Over.' Control gives us the simple code for course to steer and distance to go to reach base.

At that moment there is a flame in the sky about two miles away to our left, as a Heinkel ignites a flying bomb. The enemy aircraft is clearly illuminated as it banks away to port and Mac gets a contact as soon as I head towards it.

'Down and to port, hard,' he raps. 'Down, down, keep turning . . . steady the turn. Range one mile and still going below us. Down. Faster, you're overtaking but he's beginning to merge with the ground returns.'

By this time we are down to 500ft and, scared of overshooting, I have the throttles three-quarters open nevertheless. The sky is completely black ahead and there is no horizon; how I wish for a radio altimeter such as we have on one or two of our Mosquitos. I go on losing height until 250ft is showing on the altimeter, then 200ft and finally 150. I have to hope that the barometric pressure hasn't changed in favour of Sir Isaac, and force myself to go lower; I still can't see the sea, nor will I until we hit it at this rate.

'Any idea how high we are?' I ask when I can get a word into Mac's commentary. The AI can give some sort of indication of height, although Mk IV is better at this than Mk VIII.

'Bloody low. Range is coming down, now 3,000ft but I'm losing him in the mush at this height. You'll have to increase speed if you want to keep him.'

I open the throttles wide but the echo finally disappears in the ground returns which, even on Mk VIII, tend to be obstructive at such low altitudes. We lose that one, but our earlier success is confirmed by a Mosquito of 125 Squadron and by an air/sea rescue Walrus which happens to be passing.

There are reporters at dispersal in some peculiar way. They latch on to me like leeches and seem interested only in my age. I spend most of the time trying to convince them that the difficult part of the night's entertainment has been done by Mac, but they won't listen. The Daily Telegraph, of which my father is now air correspondent, next day publishes a paragraph about our Heinkel on the front page (not put there by him)—not a word about Mac.

Our success is not greeted with screams of applause by 125 Squadron, who reckon we have been pinching their Huns (particularly as this one was doing 140mph and the Mosquito could have coped quite all right).

Mac and I have a hasty night-flying supper in the Coltishall mess and fly home first thing afterwards.

'Congratulations, Jerry.' The Scottish burr of Tommy from flying control greets us on the R/T as we reach Ford at dawn. 'Do you want me to ring up your dispersal and say you are on your way?'

'No thanks, Tommy. I'll do it myself,' I reply before putting the Beau into fine pitch, opening the taps and making a fast low run over the groundcrew hut. The Beaufighter was christened 'Whispering Death' by the Japanese, because it gives absolutely no warning of its approach low down like this, until it roars overhead like the clap of doom. The erks know from this tactic that we have had success, because we never beat up dispersal on any other occasion, so they are quickly out looking the aircraft over for damage and grabbing a little reflected excitement. Their lives are dull enough, with cold engines to service at all times of the day and night, so Mac and I spend a few minutes chatting with them before going into the dispersal hut. The aircraft has worked, the engines have worked, the AI has worked, the radio has worked, the guns have worked (but the armourer is inside the aircraft already and finds that we have had a stoppage in the starboard outer after fifteen rounds; he cannot resist announcing this and is immediately the butt of his comrades, all of whose equipment gave no trouble).

We go home to the mess and climb into bed as everyone else is getting up, having set the cardboard clocks on the outside of our doors for calls at one o'clock.

The unit had one more success with the Beaufighter when Bill Maguire shot down another V1-carrying Heinkel later in the month. After that Fighter Command decided to call off the experiment on the grounds that the Beaufighter would not be resurrected anyway, so there was no point in getting the resident Mosquito crews' backs up. We continued to pursue the HE 111s to their lairs by flying intruder operations to Zwischenahn, Aalhorn and Münster, where they were operating. Mac and I went in November to no avail. Besides nearly fifty hours on defensive patrols, this was our twentieth offensive sortie, but we had reason to believe that our quieter trips were not counted as religiously as those of Bomber Command. We said nothing, although I had noticed a resurgence of the old symptoms recently. It was not so much that I had become noticeably jumpy to my knowledge, but that I found my flying skill was declining. Whenever we landed back after an intruder, or any other long flight which had perhaps been dogged by bad weather, I got the aircraft down all right but the old polish wasn't there. We were beginning to bounce on landing, hitting with one wheel first or levelling off too high. The funny thing was that I knew we were going to do it but could do absolutely nothing about it. In the end I would just tell Mac to hold on to his hat and reckon that any landing you could walk away from was a good one. I began to think that, after all, the system of six months' rest between tours of operations was a good idea.

Navigators, of course, had no control over the aircraft in which they were flying, and thus were entirely in the hands of their pilot. Mac, therefore, had a double ration of anxiety at work for, besides the stresses I have tried to show were in every-one's background, he now had to wonder whether perhaps one day I might run out of flying speed on the approach, or make an error of judgement in bad weather and fly into a 'stuffed cloud' (high ground covered by cloud). I'm glad I was a pilot.

The war was going so well at this stage that it was obvious that it could not last much longer. So much so that FIDS decided to reserve a table for twelve for Victory Night whenever that should be. It is much to the credit of the Crown at Chidding-fold, one of our favourite haunts, that they accepted this rather vague booking of ours.

We still had to keep going on the various trials which Fighter Command arranged for us. Although AI Mk X had now been in squadron service for quite a while, there were various supplementary trials with it to keep us occupied. Apart from the gyro gunsight ranging of which I have already written, there were trials with paint applied to the underside of the perspex nose to try and cut out such ground returns as were caused by spillage over the lip of the reflector. I was to remember these trials with advantage ten years later. The Meteor nightfighter squadrons in 83 Group, where I was on the head-quarters staff in Germany, started complaining of excessive ground returns on their AI Mk X and we turned up the relevant CFE report. At the time, however, the Mosquito was given what was called a universal nose, which was a perspex radome designed to accept AI's Mk VIII, IX, X and XV or *ASH*, and we had to see that it didn't affect performance of the aircraft or the radar. At this time also AI Mk XIV, or AIA, was undergoing trials and we also had sophisticated versions of *Perfectos* (now giving better range on Luftwaffe IFF equipment) and *Monica* in the unit. We were also suddenly presented with the North American Black Widow for evaluation. This twin-engined aircraft was specially developed by the United States for night fighting and was equipped with SCR 720, or AI Mk X as we called it. The aircraft was too heavy and we didn't like it. In addition, almost everything was controlled by electricity so that a failure of ancillary items was quite likely. On my first solo in the brute, a navigator who had come along for the ride (not Mac) unknowingly knocked a master switch with his elbow as he stood behind me. As a result I found that I could not alter the airscrew pitch and, despite looking every-where in case just this sort of thing had happened, we failed to find it, so I had to make a landing without being able to vary propeller speed. This was not a serious problem in itself, but it was a pointer to a general failing.

9 HARRYING THE HUN

In December Chris Hartley was promoted to group captain to fill the vacant post at the top of the Night Fighter Development Wing. His place as CO was taken by Bill Maguire, who had been doing the job of Squadron Leader Ops, which I now found myself moved into. This meant less contact with day-to-day flying arrangements and much more desk work, for I became responsible for drafting and producing the unit's reports, the most pressing of which was the one on AI Mk IX. Flight Lieutenant Hedgcoe and Flying Officer Norman Bamford (the same Bamford whom we had taken as an airman from the special signals section of 604 Squadron and trained on the squadron to be an RO) left us to go to 151 Squadron, where Hedgie was to take over a flight with the rank of squadron leader. They were killed on their first flight at their new job, when their aircraft inexplicably ran foul of Sir Isaac while coming in to land at Hunsdon; a six months' rest from operations would probably have saved their lives. I was glad to welcome 'Togs' Mellersh, who had come back on the disbandment of 96 Squadron.

23 December 1944
I fly Gerald Maxwell's son in the station Tiger Moth. He is a cadet in the Air Training Corps and is home for the Christmas holidays.

1 January 1945
Mac managed to get a bottle of Scotch last night so that we could celebrate Hogmanay properly. The Luftwaffe surprised everyone this morning by staging an offensive daylight sweep on our airfields on the

Continent. They flew about 750 sorties at dawn and accounted for nearly 200 of our aircraft on the ground; German losses were also more than 200, so it wasn't very successful from their point of view.

The unit then received what was probably the world's first airborne GCI set. This was a Coastal Command Wellington, in which the 10cm *ASV* (Air to Surface Vessel radar) had been modified so that it would give good responses from low-flying aircraft when the Wellington was low down, and also so that the top of the CRT always pointed north whatever course the Wellington was steering. This GCI aircraft also had an *Eureka* radar beacon in the tail, which showed up on AIs Mk VIII and X, so that one or more nightfighters could follow easily behind, ready to be given interception instructions by the controller sitting in the Wellington. The idea was to extend the low-seeing radar coverage of the North Sea so that the HE 111s which were air-launching flying bombs could be intercepted farther out. The operation was code-named *Vapour* and trials were started before the end of the year.

2 January 1945
Mac and I fly one of the new Mosquito 30s on operation Vapour. *Intelligence had told us that the Hun was coming but they had forgotten to tell the Hun. The 30 is a heavy aircraft, even when fuel tanks are nearly empty; approach speed is 150 and you come over the hedge at 130mph.*

5 January 1945
Operation Vapour *again. We take a Beau this time and are scrambled from Coltishall. We are too late and, anyway, the Wimpy's ASV is u/s. Thank God we have a radio altimeter this time and have done some practice in daylight to convince us of its reliability. We fly in the dark at 50ft (fairly) happily.*

8 January 1945
The MT section gives a dance to which I am invited. I have a few jugs

in the mess before going over to the ballroom and, on going outside the door, find the service motorbike of some despatch rider propped against the wall. The entrance to the ballroom contains no steps but a convenient ramp as I well know, so I decide that the proper thing would be to turn up to the motor transport dance on service motor transport. The bike starts first kick and soon I am wending my way down the passage to the dance. The band is playing as I arrive and I am genuinely surprised that everybody stops dancing at my rather noisy entrance; I had expected to mingle with the dancers. I ride up to the MT officer and ask him to sign the Form 658 authorising my journey in service transport; he grins nervously and hopes I won't exceed the camp speed limit in the ballroom. After one triumphant circuit I have the sense to ride out again before I break anything. The visit appears to be popular with the MT types, who all want to buy me more beer when I get back, on foot this time.

Twenty years later I was to ask Tortington Hall girls school about a place there for my 10-year-old daughter, citing as one of my qualifications for sending her there that I had ridden a motor cycle round their ballroom.

13 January 1945
Operation Vapour. *A Beaufighter and AI Mk VIII again, but this time using Manston as our advanced base. We take-off and latch on behind the Wimpy, then stooge out towards the Dutch coast together. Our tame boffin, E. J. Smith, has worked out a patrol so that the Wimpy can guarantee to cover a Heinkel flying at 150mph if it crosses out of Holland between certain points. If the Wimpy has started its northward leg and just misses the Heinkel as it enters the area, we shall be back again on the southward leg before the Hun has flown out of the vital zone. We patrol for a short while and are then ordered off the 'tow line' and given an interception.*

'*We have several customers,' says the controller happily. All seems to be working and the weather is playing its part. Calm enough to let us fly at under 100ft, with a nice trace of horizon; not that I look out of the cockpit at that height, having my eyes glued to my instruments to make sure that I don't stray too low, or slip height a little on the turn.*

'*All targets are flying west and we have chosen one for you. He is crossing to port, range one mile.' Never have I felt the clinical nature of an interception more keenly than tonight: we know for certain that our target is hostile and he has been selected for execution.*

'*Contact,' calls Mac. 'Turn port gently. Range 4,000ft. Target slightly above.'*

As soon as he has stabilised the situation and is prepared to continue the interception without further help, I call the airborne controller and pass him the appropriate code word.

'*Judy* [code word signifying 'satisfactory AI contact. We will continue the interception ourselves']. *37 out.*'

I switch on the amplified intercom, which shuts out all R/T so that Mac can continue his patter uninterrupted. The target turns north for some strange reason, but we close happily. Eventually I can see it and we close to 150yd and about 60° up. It's a bloody Wellington. I look again and make Mac get the Ross night glasses on it, willing it to be a Heinkel. But it's a Wimpy all right so we don't waste any more time on it.

On calling our own Wellington, we are told that all other trade has gone westwards and that we are to return to patrol position. And that is the nearest we get to the Luftwaffe that night. The Heinkels are certainly over, and it's just bad luck that the controller chose the one and only friendly aircraft from all the blips he had on his tube. Our jinx is operating again.

This, in fact, represented the end of the air-launching effort. KG.53, the unit involved, was withdrawn next night for lack of fuel and bases. It had lost seventy-seven aircraft during its short period of operations (including those lost by III KG.3, the Gruppe on which the full Geschwader was formed); of this total, only sixteen were shot down and the remainder were the result of Sir Isaac's influence. He operated with fine impartiality on both sides and must have found the extremely low-flying unit a temptation impossible to resist.

5 February 1945
I am struggling with the AI Mk IX report when I get a letter handed to

me by Bill, now resplendent in the CO's office, next door to mine as Squadron Leader Ops. It is from the C-in-C Fighter Command congratulating me on the award of the DFC. This decoration has been given to so many aircrew that it has really become a kind of campaign medal, which you get if you complete two tours of operations and keep your nose clean (and survive). So I am absolutely delighted to have got it and very proud, but my joy is badly marred when I learn that there is no similar letter for Mac. Whatever I have done he has done too and I am sure Chris Hartley will have put him up for a decoration at the same time as he put me up. This is yet another example of discrimination against navigators; what do we have to do to get him his gong? I feel dreadful and almost ashamed when I see Mac for the first time, but he is so obviously delighted for me that I cannot go on being silly about it.

10 February 1945
Barbara is posted to the north of England. I reckon she will leave many a broken heart behind her (my own will yearn a bit).

14 February 1945
More than 1,100 aircraft attacked Dresden last night and only five were lost. This is a measure of the domination we have achieved over the German night defences. Mosquitos hound the German nightfighters from take-off to touch-down: while they are flying to the bomber stream, over their assembly beacons, in the stream, over the target and back at their airfields again. Every time they switch on their Lichtenstein *or* SN2 *they are liable to be homed on; their IFF is triggered to provide further evidence of their presence. R/T communication with the ground is either blotted out or else false orders are given by German-speaking RAF controllers monitoring their frequencies.*

The Luftwaffe defences are frequently fooled, by spoof raids, into mistaking the target until it is too late; sometimes a small force of 20–30 Mosquito bombers is all that flies over Germany, yet the full defence system is forced into action as jammers and Window *make it look like the real thing. Even when they succeed in intercepting an aircraft, it might turn out to be a Mosquito nightfighter intent on turning the tables. On returning to land, the Luftwaffe pilots are forced to fly at nought feet to escape the attentions of the inevitable Mosquito, which relentlessly patrols every night-flying airfield.*

Of course, last night's success might be because the enemy wasn't expecting a mass raid on such a peaceful town as Dresden, where they only seem to make porcelain as far as I can see.

It was small wonder that the Luftwaffe credited the Mosquito with almost legendary powers. All losses, whether from bad weather, enemy action or operational fatigue were put down to the attentions of the RAF's wooden wizard. By this time there was no such thing in the Luftwaffe as a posting off operations, so that they suffered far worse attacks of the 'twitch' than we ever did, and their 'chop' rate from accidents was almost as high as their battle casualties.

15 February 1945
Somebody somewhere has evidently come up with the idea that the Germans might use gas as a last resort. So we are to run some trials to see whether the standard oxygen mask is sufficient protection to enable air-craft to operate. A cloud of tear gas is released at the upwind end of Tangmere runway, and FIDS lands and takes-off in it without any trouble. This doesn't prove anything as the concentration apparently wasn't sufficient.

We were doing a Mk IX exercise two days later and Bill Maguire was up with Denis Lake at the same time, trying out an attitude indicator which had recently arrived and been installed in a Mosquito. We both landed into a greater concentration of gas than last time, with oxygen masks tightly fitting and oxygen on full flow. Neither of us had any trouble and then Mac and I went off for our Mk IX trials. When we got down it was with horror that we learned that Bill and Denis were dead. They were seen to do a roll fairly low down (unlike Bill but not, in itself, necessarily dangerous) followed by another, rather slow and badly executed (very unlike Bill, who was an excellent pilot). This was immediately followed by a flick roll as the aircraft's nose dropped; they then half straightened out before hitting the ground just beyond the airfield. I had flown the aircraft the day before and we had been encouraged to examine the attitude indicator carefully during abnormal positions. Bill was presumably watching it as he rolled onto his back and so lost flying speed. This was a tragedy which hit us all for, not only was Bill the CO and a much liked and respected pilot, but Denis Lake had been with us for a long time and his quiet dedication to his task had made him a popular figure with all ranks.

17 February 1945
'Batchy' Atcherly comes over to have a drink and commiserate with us. Among others I get screeching and finish the evening by putting my arm round the air commodore's shoulders.

'There's something I want to say to you, sir,' I say, a trifle thickly. 'I hope you won't take it amiss.'

'No, Jerry,' he replies. 'Whatever it is, go ahead and say it.'

So I straighten up, holding myself as steady as possible, and look him squarely in the eye.

'Hiya, "Batchy",' I say solemnly and collapse with helpless laughter.

Gonsalves, ex-604 and 85 Squadrons, came to take over the unit and he brought his infectious brand of humour with him, plus an undoubted ability to fly through worse weather than almost anyone else.

We went on flogging the gas trials and I see that Mac and I landed at Tangmere quite a few times over the next three or four days. On one occasion my logbook says 'Mark IX (u/s) and gas. Mac screeching!' I can but suppose that we went after lunch and that my Scotsman, after imbibing well, had made an exception to the rule and had forced himself on me for the flight. Small wonder the AI was u/s.

23 February 1945
Fighter Command has decided that it would be a good idea for all aircrew

*to spend a day in a flying control tower, just to see how it works. We are
already on excellent terms with our flying controllers and frequently pop
in and out (especially as they have some good-looking WAAFs there) but
we must obey so, as second in command, I start the ball rolling.*

*I am standing on the balcony outside the glass control office when Alan
Sutcliff and Jimmy Barrow take-off in a Mosquito. As it passes the
control building I can see smoke coming from the starboard engine,
which is obviously failing, and the aircraft, equally obviously, hasn't got
single-engine flying speed.*

*'He's going to crash!' I call into the control office. 'He's going to
crash!'*

*There is evidently an urgency in my voice because Tommy doesn't wait
to check for himself, but pushes the panic button without further ado. The
alarm bell rings, ambulance and fire engine scramble from their garages
and people pour out onto the balcony.*

*With a sinking heart I watch the Mosquito trailing smoke and not
gaining height, until it disappears behind some trees. A column of oily
black smoke curls up to the sky about three miles away as the crash
tenders roar off into the countryside, and then there is silence; there is no
reply to our calls on the R/T.*

I go into the building, find a chair and sit down.

*'Are you all right, sir?' A WAAF has been studying my face and now
brings me a cup of tea; she seems surprised that the dashing young
squadron leader complete with shining new DFC ribbon should have gone
white and needed to sit down. But I know what will have been happening
in the cockpit as Alan struggled to gain speed and height. My cursed
imagination can picture vividly what can happen as the Mosquito
ploughs through hedges, trees and buildings. I know all too well what
that column of black smoke means. Her mind is placid with ignorance.*

Alan got away with cuts and bruises in the ensuing crash but
Jimmy Barrow was badly burned about the face. A week later I
went to visit him in the burns unit of Dr Archibald McIndoe's
hospital at East Grinstead, where hundreds of aircrew—the
famous 'guinea-pigs'—were patched up with skin grafts and
plastic surgery, for which work he received a well-deserved

knighthood after the war. It wasn't a pleasant experience to look into the shattered faces of men being slowly rebuilt by skill, patience and their own courage, but it was important not to show revulsion and I was glad to have made the journey.

The order requiring us to send a pilot or navigator to flying control every day was withdrawn.

3 March 1945

We have the party to end all parties in the Officers' Mess at Tortington Hall. A hard-working committee has spent two weeks working on preparations and the ballroom looks fabulous, with candle-lit tables and hidden lighting. Barbara comes down for it, of course, and the top brass and brains of the nightfighter world are all assembled from Fighter Command, 11 Group and 100 Group. In the middle of it all Chris Hartley, who has been saving it all day for this moment, calls for silence and announces to general acclaim the award of the DFC to Mac. He is made to go up to the stage and have a ribbon which somebody has produced pinned on his breast. Violette is there to see his moment of glory and I find a most unmilitary lump in my throat.

We have a fantastic time—and so does the Hun. He chooses this night to despatch more than a hundred nightfighters on intruder attacks against Bomber Command airfields in East Anglia; they shoot down twenty-two of our aircraft.

I am in my office next day, which happens to be a Sunday, when the telephone starts ringing first thing and seems to go on all morning, as various HQs try to contact their Night Ops staff.

'No. Group Captain Hiscox wasn't down to breakfast when I left the Mess at eight o'clock . . .'

'Yes. Group Captain Cunningham has already left by air for Northolt . . .'

'No. Air Commodore Chisholm is at Mass I understand . . .'

'Yes. Squadron Leader Rawnsley is with Group Captain Cunningham . . .'

'Yes. Wing Commander Davison is in the Mess . . .'

This sudden activity on the part of the Luftwaffe was followed up in a small way the next night, but our defences were not caught napping a second time; twenty German aircraft were shot down. Hitler thereupon once more intervened to stop further sorties of this nature on the grounds that the results could not be seen by the German people.

5 March 1945
Fly Barbara back to Ouston in a Mosquito. I choose the occasion to make my ritziest landing ever—all three wheels touch down together so smoothly that I literally don't know when we reach the ground. This is the only time I have ever done this and is a complete fluke and wasted on Barbara, who probably thinks that all landings are like that always.

AI Mk IX took up a lot of our effort now, but we still found time to try out an imitation of the German upward-firing *Schräge Musik* in dummy night attacks on a Lancaster of the Bomber Development Unit; further trials of AIA (Mk XIV); of *Hookah*, which was a wide-band homer for which the scientists wanted a polar diagram; trials on *Monica* rear warners (the Mk VIII version by now); and *Perfectos* homer on German IFF.

I managed to fix a 48-hour pass for my twenty-third birthday and went home to Bath. While I was walking in civilian clothes in the local village with my mother, she was asked about Peter's progress by an acquaintance.

'And you're Jeremy I suppose,' went on the well-meaning inquisitor. 'How does it feel to have a hero for a brother? The war will be over before you can get to it.'

'I'll have you know he's a squadron leader,' bridled my mother before I could stop her. 'And he's just been awarded the DFC.'

This completed my embarrassment but must have given my mother a proud moment.

17 March 1945
Micky and Smithy are missing from an intruder.

They were shot down by the combined efforts of an RAF

bomber whom they were investigating and a German night-fighter which was investigating them both. They were made prisoners of war.

20 March 1945
The unbelievable has happened! Some pipsqueak at Air Ministry has taken it upon himself to write to CFE noting that 'Flt. Lt. MacRae requested to be trained for flying in 1942 so that he could go on operations'. The pompous pen-pusher goes on to say that it would appear that the said Flt. Lt. MacRae has been in a non-operational unit ever since he was awarded his flying badge, and isn't it about time he did some of the ops he professed to be so keen to do? This is almost libellous, but we are certain that Chris Hartley can rise to the occasion with a caustic reply, not forgetting to mention Mac's DFC—earned non-operationally of course.

21 March 1945
The unbelievable has happened again! Elizabeth has been promoted to second officer. We all thought that she was destined to become the Navy's longest-serving third officer. But she'll never make it to admiral!

27 March 1945
I fly our new Meteor Mk III with Welland IIB engines; it smells heavily of paraffin. My log book says: 'First solo on type and first flight in a jet job. Not all that impressive.'

28 March 1945
I fly an ME 110. My log books says: 'First solo on type. A wizard job.' The 110 is rather like a twin-engined Tiger Moth to fly, simple and uncomplicated, and I thoroughly enjoy myself.

Two days later I flew the JU 88, which was an interesting air-craft but, although faster and better than the ME 110 for night fighting, not such an easy aeroplane to fly.

There followed more AI Mk IX as the pressure increased to get out our report. We were flying our solitary Mosquito with this radar every day and every night. On 7 April we suddenly discovered that our Meteor was serviceable and needed to be flown at night so that someone could look at its exhausts and see how bright they were. We were in the middle of a session in the bar at the time, but Bill Howell of the Navigator Leaders School was as ready to help out as I was to fly anything anywhere. We rushed down to the dispersal in a haze of gin and leaped into the air to look at the Meteor from the AI Mk IX Mosquito before anybody could stop us. This was the only occasion on which I ever flew after drinking more than a pint of beer, and we felt very pleased with ourselves that night, although in fact we were rather silly.

On 12 April I was just putting the finishing touches to the report on AI Mk IX, when news came through that Mac and I had both been posted. He was promoted to squadron leader and posted to the nightfighter OTU at Charterhall; I was to go to Night Ops at HQ 11 Group, Uxbridge, with John and Jimmy, to start an intruder section. Together Mac and I had flown more than forty operational sorties with FIU, split about half and half between offensive and defensive patrols. This brought my personal operational flying to something over 325 hours, stretching continuously over a period of more than three years; I could not complain at being rested. I naturally flew Mac to Charterhall when he went up there on 13 April and we parted with similar feelings, I suspect. We had been through much together and, while we could not point to a long string of victories to our credit, we had each waged and won a private war; we had also turned our hands to many tasks and not disgraced ourselves. We had forged a friendship in the fire of a common experience, which nothing can ever take away from either of us. Mac had wrestled with his conscience when he was on a safe ground job, where he could easily have stayed throughout the war. Instead he chose the way of honour and I helped him in his search to be able to live with himself after the war.

When he is so taciturn and modest, how do I know all this?

Because he presented me with a book when we parted and, on the flyleaf, was written:

'Thanks, Jerry, for more than you'll ever know.'

5 May 1945

It is obvious that the war is nearly over. Today is Saturday and we have a premature peace party at 11 Group Headquarters; Peter comes as my guest. The party is much like many others, only more so, and is chiefly memorable for the fact that A. H. Andrew is also there, masquerading as an intelligence officer. This imposing figure, who was our housemaster when we were both at Felsted School before the war, is now a flight lieutenant and thus junior to us, as squadron leaders. He submits good-humouredly as we stand one at each end of the anteroom and march him up and down between us.

VE Day was 8 May. I went in the morning to the local church service in Uxbridge, which was chiefly memorable for the fact that the vicar spent half his sermon telling us that there should have been more of us there. I felt that he should have been saying that outside in the street and not to those of us who were already inside; and I nearly got up and told him so. The service ended with the National Anthem and, when it came to the fourth line, there was a suitable roll from the organ and I had a second or two to think of the implications of the line. To my surprise I found that my voice let me down and the line choked in my throat—a sensation I can still recall vividly today at the same line if I let my mind fly back to that day.

That evening I was in the 11 Group officers' mess having the first of what would undoubtedly be many drinks, when I was called to the telephone. It was FIDS. Did I want to celebrate the peace with them? There was a bed in the mess at Ford for as long as I cared to stay. Would I like to join them?

Would I? I couldn't think why I hadn't thought of it myself. All flying was temporarily banned, so I jumped into my Alvis two-seater sports car and headed south for the friends I had known so long. We had one long party stretching over four or five days, starting at the Crown at Chiddingfold, where they duly honoured the open booking we had made in December for a table for VE night.

As I drove back to Uxbridge when it was all over, I thought of all that had happened over the last five years, and knew that my decisions could not with peace of mind have been other. I recalled the misery and mud of airfield defence, the thrill of my first solo, the temptation to stay in Canada as an instructor, the fear of fire as Tony and I slithered to a halt on our belly in a Blenheim. The frustration of that first fast JU 88 low over the North Sea came vividly to mind, as did the gnawing feeling in the pit of my stomach while we twisted and turned to escape the 'whirling spray' at Rheine. I remembered the awful sights of Hanover, Frankfurt and the Ruhr under fire as we circled and searched for enemy nightfighters; the satisfaction of our first enemy aircraft destroyed; the sheer hard grind of instrument flying when I was tired and my senses refused to believe what the blind-flying panel told them, while ice and St Elmo's Fire did their best to distract my concentration. I recalled the announcement of Mac's DFC at the dance, having to force myself to fly lower and yet lower over the North Sea when there was no horizon and no radio altimeter, having to fight off the attentions of Sir Isaac Newton as we scratched into Ford in rain and bad visibility, and too long a list of names and faces I would see no more.

I thought of my brother Peter, now a squadron leader at a group headquarters and of the crews I had known with slight accents in their voices, who had brought a hint of the wide-open spaces of their motherlands with them, volunteers all from Australia and New Zealand, from South Africa and Rhodesia and from Canada and Bermuda. None of the Dominions had been forced to come to our help and they must have known what they were letting themselves in for, because their fathers had done the same in 1914–18. This will eventually come to be recognised as among the most magnificent sacrifices of history and I wondered whether we hadn't, perhaps, taken them rather for granted. I had also met, and admired, a lot of Americans and Norwegians.

I was glad the killing and the danger were over and I hoped that somebody would build on the mutual trust and respect we had formed for each other.

My stock of material treasure was not high, but not for all the gold in Pharaoh's tomb would I have changed one second of those five years. No, not any of the time spent shivering in my dinghy, nor when forcing myself to climb ever upwards towards the towering black menace blotting out the whole eastern sky, nor when my heels literally drummed on the cockpit floor in momentary terror at the thought of the enemy on our tail, nor even when we realised that we were flying at 1,500ft alone over Cologne so that we received the undivided attention of the German defences.

I had waged my private struggle and had won it. More, I had been vouchsafed a glimpse of Olympia and, for a short while, I too had lived among the Gods.

10   POSTSCRIPT

They say that you should never go back but when, twenty years after it was all over and I was in the yachting business, I heard that someone was building boats at Ford, I couldn't resist the temptation to go and see them.

The last few miles brought memories flooding: the garage where you were sometimes good for a coupon-free gallon; the wall, still scarred from the impact of Teddy's car, and which he had excused by saying that he had thought it was a hedge; the police station where we had 'liberated' our first VE Day flag; the girls' school which had been our officers' mess.

Gravel crunched under the wheels as my car came to a stop. The front door had had a coat of paint since our day. The bar had been just inside on the right—probably the headmistress's study now (did the walls ever echo the words of 'Eskimo Nell'?); the new wing contained the bedrooms, and there was the ballroom where we had held that famous party and the Luftwaffe had come over in strength—and Mac's DFC had been announced to general acclaim.

Under the uninterested eye of a gardener sweeping leaves in the autumn sunlight, I turned the car and beat a retreat to continue up to the airfield. A prison now bestrides the road which runs through the camp; barbed wire coils its way along a high fence, keeping out the visitor as effectively as it presumably keeps in the inmates. But further reconnaissance revealed that there was an entry through the old fuel installation in the south-west dispersal.

A farmer was busy with his tractor on the land between the runways, overlooked by the sightless stare of the glass observation hut on top of the flying-control tower, where I was standing on the day that Jimmy Barrow crashed on take-off and was so badly burned.

'Hello, Cheapjack 37.' Tommy's accent came loud and clear from the past. 'This is Lighthouse. You are clear to taxi.'

The car stole onto the perimeter track and instinctively my hand groped for the Mosquito's throttles. Weeds grew unchecked through cracks in the tarmac. Half a lifetime fell away as I moved at taxiing pace towards the old dispersal, untenanted and beckoning on the far side of the airfield. Past the spot where the ME 108 had belly landed at dawn with escaping Czechs; past the end of the runway where I had had to land on one engine two nights in a row; past the dispersal where a crippled Lancaster had ploughed through four of our aircraft.

It was like coming home. The squadron office, with its nonstandard bay window installed by Rory Chisholm in the days when building permission was even more difficult to obtain than it is now, still tried to give an air of spacious comfort where none prevailed. A nick in the door bore mute testimony to a flying inkwell when 'Togs' had had to duck to avoid the consequence of a particularly facetious remark.

The adjutant's office and orderly room each contributed its share of atmosphere, and then I was wandering past the hangars, gaunt skeletons shuttered against the world, with their broken windows catching the splintered sunlight high up near the roof.

The remains of our dispersal hut still contained the stove. Silent and brooding, it stared distrustfully from a gaping maw, remembering its nightly mixture of coke, paraffin and signal cartridges. I poked my head round the door of the airmen's crewroom.

'Sar'nt Boarer! Scramble Mosquito 360!'

The only answer was the slam of a door farther inside. It creaked and slammed again, echoing down the years. Back came the beat of a thousand Merlins, the myriad curses of a generation of groundcrew and the sickly, delicious taste of hot sweet tea and condensed milk at four in the morning.

It took some time to find my way into the maintenance hangar. After pushing through grass to my waist, I at length found a door which reluctantly responded to my probing fingers. I stepped inside and paused. The sun's rays slanted down from the broken skylights, past the roof girders, to form a lattice pattern of shadows on the floor. My imagination conjured voices from the past: Wing Commander Wood and our bridge player, Bill Maguire and Teddy Daniel, Hedgie and Joe Berry ('Carry on chaps, I've had it.'), until I could actually hear them whispering to me through the rafters. The sound was so clear that the hairs on the back of my neck rose and slowly I took another, hesitant, step forward.

The whisper became louder, turned to a rustle and then to the sudden metallic clatter of wings that betrayed the presence of twenty or thirty pigeons. It was only then that I noticed the pathetic corpses which littered the floor.

The birds had evidently found their way in through the broken windows and were now trapped. Starvation had overtaken some, while the rest continued to beat senselessly against the glass. It seemed that Sir Isaac Newton still held a mortgage on this piece of property, payable as always by the unwary.

I found the lorry door and fought it for five minutes before it yielded and creaked open. I wedged it and went back to the car to wait.

After five minutes the first bird shot out of the opening and curved steeply up towards the blue sky. After a moment or two it was followed by another. I started the engine and drove quietly away.

'Hello Cheapjack 37, this is Lighthouse calling. Your pigeons are 080, thirty miles.'

That is how the controller would have given the bearing and distance of Ford from my house that night. But I had retired from the Royal Air Force by then and I was glad I had let them go.

Now I am old and going grey. Occasionally I look back across the years, and my eye brightens and my head sits a little higher on my shoulders as I recall how Tony, Mac and I flew with Fighter Command.

The memories were not achieved without an effort of will at times. Nobody will ever be able to take them away.

GLOSSARY OF CODE WORDS, INITIALS AND SERVICE TERMS

Code words are in italics

Abdullah	Operation to home on Würzburg radar transmissions just prior to D-Day (British).
AFDU	Air Fighting Development Unit (day-fighter equivalent of FIU).
AI	Airborne Interception (radar).
Mk IV	1½m. Fixed dipole aerials with 'floodlighting' principle. Range limited to height.
Mk V	As Mk IV but with pilot indication.
Mk VI	As Mk V, but installed in single-seater fighter.
Mk VII	10cm with spirally rotating scanner. Max range 5–6 miles, even when low down, because of beamed transmissions.
Mk VIII	As Mk VII but with beacon and IFF facilities. Max range 7–8 miles.
Mk IX	10cm, having spiral scanner with ability to lock onto target. Windscreen projection of target blip and of instruments. Max range 10 miles.
Mk X	10cm, with fully rotating scanner. Max range 10 miles.
Mk XV	3cm, with horizontal scanner. Max range 8 miles. Also called *ASH* and used by Royal Navy.
A-scope	CRT showing side view of target on linear time base.
ASH	AI Mk XV.
ASV	Air to Surface Vessel (airborne radar in 10cm band).
BABS	Blind Approach Beacon System (using radar).

BDU	Bomber Development Unit (bomber equivalent of FIU).
Beechnut	British device to communicate with aircraft through R/T jamming.
Blip	Radar echo or response.
Bogey	Unidentified aircraft (British).
B-scope	CRT showing plan view of target.
Canopy exercise	Searchlight practice over an airfield (British).
CFE	Central Fighter Establishment.
CH	Chain Home (British early warning radar).
CHL	Chain Home Low.
CHEL	Chain Home Extra Low.
Corkscrew	Standard evasion developed for use by British bombers over enemy territory. It involved flying in a horizontal spiral rather like a corkscrew. The extended corkscrew doubled each deviation from course and was extremely difficult for nightfighters to follow on AI.
CRT	Cathode-Ray Tube.
C-scope	CRT showing front elevation of target.
Düppel	German code name for their equivalent of *Window*.
Emil Emil	German R/T code name for *Lichtenstein* AI.
ESN	Enemy Signal Number (British copy of German signal cartridge).
ETA	Expected Time of Arrival.
Eureka	British radar beacon in 10cm waveband.
FIDS	Fighter Interception Development Squadron (revised name for FIU after incorporation into CFE).
FIU	Fighter Interception Unit (development unit for all forms of airborne radar used by Fighter Command by day and night, but principally by night).
Flensburg	German device to enable their nightfighters to home onto British *Monica* transmissions.
Flower	British low-level night-intruder patrol of German airfields.
Freelance	Patrol with the object of picking up a chance contact or visual on the enemy.
Freya	German early warning radar, used in conjunction with *Würzburg* to control Luftwaffe nightfighters.
GCI	Ground Controlled Interception (British radar equipment for the control of fighters).
Gee	British device for navigating by a radar grid system.

Ground return	The heavy and intense echoes received by a radar set from the ground; also known in a static radar (eg a GCI) as the permanent echo.
Himmelbett	German system of radar and control for night fighting.
H2D	A British 10cm experimental radar for detecting movement on land.
H2S	A British 10cm bombing aid, giving a representation of the countryside below the aircraft.
IFF	Identification Friend or Foe. A British device designed to code the echo sent back to a friendly AI or GCI set.
Intercom	Intercommunication. A small set which shut out the R/T and gave better communication between pilot and navigator. A running commentary could thus be given without a background of other R/T traffic.
Judy	British code word meaning 'I have AI contact and am taking over completion of the interception'.
Lichtenstein	First form of German AI. 53cm (490mc/s) and a narrow beam of only 25°. Max range two miles.
LMF	Lack of Moral Fibre. A euphemism for cowardice.
Lucero	British device for interrogating $1\frac{1}{2}$m beacons.
Mahmoud	British code name for high-level, bomber-support sorties.
Monica	British tail warning device operating on $1\frac{1}{2}$m.
Mother	British beacon operating on $1\frac{1}{2}$m.
Nav Rad	Navigator, radio. Later name for AI operator.
Naxburg	Portmanteau name for combination of *Naxos* and *Würzburg* when used as German defence radar.
Naxos	German homer in 10cm waveband. Nightfighters could home on H2S and AI Mk X transmissions with it.
NFIU	Naval Fighter Interception Unit.
NFT	Night Flying Test—to see that all equipment was fully serviceable.
OTU	Operational Training Unit, where pupil pilots were converted to operational aircraft and equipment.
Perfectos	British device for homing onto German IFF equipment.
Pigeons	British R/T procedural code word meaning 'base'.

The phrase 'Your pigeons are two seven zero, twenty', meant that your base airfield lies on a heading of 270° (due west) at a distance of 20 miles.

PPI — Plan Position Indicator. A CRT showing a plan view of the area swept by a particular radar.

Queen Bee — Head WAAF officer on a station, usually of flight officer rank.

Radar — The name introduced by the Americans to designate RDF or radiolocation; derived from the initials of RAdio Direction And Range.

Rhubarb — British code name for low-level offensive daylight fighter sweeps.

RO — Radio Operator; the early name for an AI operator.

R/T — Radio Telephony.

Schräge Musik — Literally translated: Slanting Music. German code name for guns firing upwards at 70° in night-fighters.

SCR 720 — Signal Corps Radio set no 720. The American designation for the 10cm AI which they developed from Sir Robert Watson-Watt's invention and which the British called AI Mk X.

SCR 729 — Signal Corps Radio set no 729. A set designed to receive radar homing beacons and IFF signals.

Seeburg plotter — A special table used by the Luftwaffe for filtering information from Freya and Würzburg radars used in the control of their nightfighters.

Serrate — A British equipment designed to home on German Lichtenstein AI transmissions.

SN2 — Later form of German AI. 330cm (85mc/s) and a wider coverage than Lichtenstein. Max range 3½–4 miles.

TFU — Telecommunications Flying Unit. This British unit carried out the early feasibility flying trials of the various radars developed by TRE.

TRE — Telecommunications Research Establishment. The collection of British scientists, which finally settled at Malvern in 1942, who did most of the research and development on radar in all its forms.

Turbinlite — AI-equipped nightfighter which shone a vast airborne searchlight on its target, so that the latter

178

	could then be shot down by a formating Hurricane (British).
Vapour	Code name for British operation involving direction of nightfighters from a specially equipped Wellington aircraft.
Vector	Direction to take in degrees magnetic.
VHF	Very High Frequency (radio).
VL	Visual Lorenz; a German system of runway approach lights and illuminated crossbars as an aid to bad-weather landing.
Wassermann	A very successful German early-warning radar.
Whiting	The manoeuvre during which a fighter allowed an enemy to approach to a certain distance astern at night before turning hard round in order to reverse the positions (British).
Wilde Sau	The use by the Germans of single-engined fighters over the target at night, relying on freelance interceptions from a running commentary aided by the lights from the fires and from searchlights.
Wimpy	The Wellington bomber's affectionate nickname, derived from the cartoon character J. Wellington Wimpy, a friend of Popeye the Sailor.
Window	British code name for the metal-foil strips which were dropped from aircraft and, if they were cut to half the length of the wavelength of the radar they were designed to jam, gave misleading echoes to 'flood' the CRT.
Würzburg	German fighter-control radar.
X-Gerät	German system of blind bombing involving an adaptation of the Lorenz landing beam and an early form of computer.
Zahme Sau	The use by the Germans of single- and twin-engined fighters fed into the bomber stream as soon as its track was properly established on the way to the target.

BIBLIOGRAPHY

Air Ministry. *Rise and Fall of the German Air Force* (1948)
Bekker, Cajus. *The Luftwaffe War Diaries* (1969)
Bishop, Edward. *Mosquito* (1972)
Chisholm, Roderick. *Cover of Darkness* (1953)
Collier, Basil. *The Battle of the V-Weapons* (1964)
Gibson, Guy, VC. *Enemy Coast Ahead* (1946)
Howard-Williams, Air Commodore E. L. *The Air is the Future Career*
    (1939)
Jubelin, Rear Admiral André. *The Flying Sailor* (1953)
Killen, John. *The Luftwaffe* (1970)
Knoke, Heinz. *I Flew for the Führer* (1953)
Price, Alfred. *Instruments of Darkness* (1967)
——. *Luftwaffe* (1970)
Johnen, William. *Duel under the Stars* (1957)
Richards, Denis and St George Saunders, Hilary. *The Royal Air
    Force 1939–45*, vols I, II and II (1953–4)
Rawnsley, C. F. and Wright, Robert. *Night Fighter* (1957)
Rowe, A. P. *One Story of Radar* (1948)
Sharp, C. Martin and Bowyer, Michael J. F. *Mosquito* (1967)

INDEX